END OF THE TRAIL

Dan Rice

❖

The Way Things Are Publications
Los Angeles

Route 66 enthusiast, permanent fixture on the iconic Santa Monica Pier, and proprietor of t-shirt retailer 66-to-Cali Inc., Dan Rice is a fully recovered Traumatic Brain Injury victim. His Hollywood life and high-paced track to a Ph.D. in Psychology was abruptly derailed in 2002 when he suffered severe brain injuries in a near-fatal car accident. His long and painful road to recovery began only after a long period of depression, anger, sadness, insomnia, vertigo, suicidal ideations, and an increasing inability to understand the world around him.

The shame and humiliation of being victim to brain injury inhibited Dan's journey to find help and only after his altered behavior sent his life spiraling into dangerous depths did he seek help and begin his difficult journey into recovery. Nearly ten years later and now recovered, Dan realizes the need for understanding in both the public and the psychology field. Brain trauma's hidden and misunderstood condition too often goes untreated resulting in anger, depression, broken families and ultimately suicide.

For every person diagnosed with breast cancer this year, five times will suffer a brain injury. With 650,000 new heart attacks annually, brain injury is up to three times more common. Prominent media sources cite the hallmark Iraq war injury now as being Traumatic Brain injury. The victims are all around, but their condition is cloaked from an unwillingness to seek help for risk of ridicule.

Dan Rice wrote *End of the Trail* to educate readers about brain injury and through his own dramatic experience, illuminate and inspire victims and their families as they struggle to claim back their loved ones from the mental darkness.

Dan Rice lives in California and can often be found driving historic Route 66 from "pier to pier".

1ST EDITION

Published by The Way Things Are Publications, Los Angeles.

Jacket design by Pacific Coast Creative, © 2011.
Jacket photography: © 2010 Jeremy Davidson.

ISBN-10: 0-9821419-1-2
ISBN-13: 978-0-9821419-1-5

Edited by Jennifer Havenner, Angela and Mark Hooper, and Julia DeGraf.

http://www.route-66-to-california.com/
http://www.waythingsarepublications.com

The Way Things Are Publications
11664 National Blvd
#401
Los Angeles, CA 90064

Printed on acid free paper. Meets all ANSI standards for archival quality paper.

Dedicated to my Parents, my Grandparents, and my Wife...whose constant love, guidance, and devotion has made all the difference in my life.

Acknowledgments

~

There are a number of people who I need to thank for making this book possible...first and foremost, and because teachers never get the credit they deserve, I'd like to thank Marc Johann, my 5th grade teacher. That may seem a bit arbitrary to some people, but thirty years ago, Marc wrote on one of my creative writing assignments that I had a talent for writing and that I should never quit using it. "If you don't use it, you'll lose it," were his words, and he had no idea how those words would carry me through so many tough times in my life. His example at that time, his strength, and his sincere belief in a ten year old kid inspired me to believe in the possibility that I could one day live the life of my dreams. Thanks Marc for getting me started on a lifelong chase of windmills. Had you not, I may never have caught one. Or two. Or three. So thank you again. You are the definition of what all teachers should strive to be.

I'd also like to thank my Grandparents. It was my Grandpa and Grandma Rice that showed how the things other people dreamt about could be my reality if I simply believed it. Their lives were a testament to that, and my Grandpa's honesty, modesty and unwillingness to be anything but decent to his fellow man were great examples to live up to. I hope the family legacy that I leave is the one he started.

To my Grandpa and Grandma Goss, I don't know where to begin. The depth of their love for me permeates to my very core, even these many years after I lost them. While I miss them deeply, I endeavor to let the goodness of who they were live on through me and in the spirit of what I do for others via Route 66. Whenever I see a train, I know they're not too far away.

My parents deserve a huge thank you. It's been said that I have my Dad's head and my Mom's heart, and on both counts, I am flattered. Though I've lived in California for nearly two decades, my Mother has never let me forget that I am her son. Your heart is as big as a house Mom, and your love for me and your belief in me has meant everything. It still does. It always will. Thank you for two decades of Sunday phone calls that I can set my watch by, and for always being supportive, no matter what its cost you. I love you.

My Dad has perhaps shaped my life like no other person. My love and respect for him has only grown through the years and his principles, integrity, and dedication to standing up for what he believes is right leaves me wondering why Superman gets all the press? Thank you Dad for being the guy I always wished I could be. You are the best example I know of what it means to be a man. Your tireless work ethic, your concern for all, and your passion to do what's best for the country and the greatest number of people (often to your own detriment), leaves me with an example I think can only be overshadowed by Christ Himself. I don't think there's a person I know who isn't aware I'm very proud to be your son.

To my wife Jessica, I can only say that none of this would have been possible without your love and support. You are the personal angel that God has sent to me, and I will never be able to fully comprehend the full extent of your goodness. You're just off the charts. I love you, sweetheart.

To the rest of my family and friends, I can only say, no man has better. Thank you for being such an instrumental part of who I am and for always keeping me close to my roots. My Step-Mom Mary, my Uncle Dave, Uncle Mark, and my cousin Bill each continue to hold huge influence over my life, and I have to pay a special mention to my guys in the "6 Squad." You know who you are and how much you mean to me.

I also want to acknowledge my former boss, Writer and Producer Billy Brown...thank you for your kindness, your concern, your care, your humor, and your friendship through the years. If God hadn't given me you, I have no idea where I'd be. I guarantee you one thing. I'm better off with you than without you. Except in Scrabble.

My former attorney Tracy Baer defied every stereotype I've ever heard about lawyers. If there were more like you, there would be no more lawyer jokes.

To Dr. Barry Ludwig at UCLA...how could one Doctor make such a difference? Thanks for putting me on the path to rehab and for your generosity through my recovery. Your decency will never be forgotten by me. Then again, I'm brain-damaged, so who knows what I'll remember tomorrow?

My guess is that no matter what, your reputation is safe.

Tammy, my former speech therapist, you showed me the grace of a willow tree swaying in the wind. Thank you for helping me get to the top of the mountain, both literally and figuratively.

To my chiropractors Dr. King Rollins and Dr. Tom Harvey, I have to say thank you for putting my back and neck back in alignment that first year after my accident. Those immediate months afterward were excruciating, and I owe both of you for getting me back on the straight and narrow and encouraging me to stay in the gym so my recovery could be quicker. That said, I want to thank my lifelong friend, personal trainer, and physical health guru Shaun Hadsall for the tough workouts and keeping me strong. You were all right. My physical recovery made my mental recovery so much easier.

To all those who opposed me, took advantage of me, or treated me badly during my recovery, God bless you. You made me stronger.

To my friend Steve Burton...your example to millions of others on "General Hospital" is more important than you know. God uses each of us in different ways, and I'm certain you've inspired more than just me to believe a full life is still possible after brain injury. Now that I've recovered, I'll stop shy of emulating your character's "hit man" profession on the show, but I'll say I do understand after a brain injury that finding a good job isn't always easy. Thanks for all you do.

To my first ever editor and publisher, Jen, I'm forever grateful to you for making this such a fun ride with "The Way Things Are" Publishing. What a great experience. I'm so happy to say that everything you prepared me for turned out to be wrong. Somehow you messed up and made this whole experience a blast. You are one of the most humble, intelligent, and entirely collaborative people I have ever known. I am blown away by what you've done. Thank you.

I also have to thank Jim Conkle of the Route 66 Alliance, Ben Franz-Knight of Pike's Place in Seattle and Mark Havenner of the Pollack PR Marketing Group. All the best things in my life have come from a springboard of friendship, and what we did together in just eight days with the "End of the Trail" is much more than unbelievable business...it's unbelievably special because I did it with my friends. Thanks for helping me start the second chapter of my life.

I also have to thank the entire Santa Monica Pier Restoration Corporation Board of Directors and the City of Santa Monica. I can never fully articulate just how thankful I am for the chance to promote such a piece of American History as Route 66 from such a piece of American History as the Santa Monica Pier. I will say this though: I can feel your support and I'm grateful. The future looks bright ahead.

This list also wouldn't be complete without a mention of my friends out in the Route 66 Community. If it wasn't for the inspiration of people like Angel Delgadillo, Jim Ross, Shellee Graham, Jerry McClanahan, Jim Hinckley, Fran Hauser and the whole crew at the Midpoint Café, not to mention folks like Nick and Demi Adam, Gary Turner, Melba Rigg, Bob and Ramona Lehman, Sandra and Don Myers, John and Karen Harvey, Allan Affeldt, John Peasley, Harley and Annabelle Russell, Laurel Kane, Kumar Patel, David Knudson, Ken Turmel, Anna Marie Dallago, Bob "Crocodile" Lyle, Ron Jones, Jim Bush, and the whole fun cast of characters up at the Victorville California Route 66 Museum, to name a few...what I do on a daily basis wouldn't be any fun without you. It's all of you folks who continue to inspire me today.

To my friend and mentor, John Chung and his ever present, devoted second-in-command Esther Park, I have to say thank God for both of you in my life. Thank you for all your prayers and for your faithful, caring guidance. Your sincerity and kindness will not easily be matched in my life. Thanks for helping me to make "66-to-Cali" a reality and for ensuring that my Grandpa's legacy lives on.

Lastly, to my Lord God in Heaven, I know that none of this story would have happened without you. I can confidently tell everyone I know that God has guided every inch of every step of the way, and He's stood by me even when I've ventured off His path only to lead me back again. While my whole life is impossible, He makes it clear that all things are possible through Him. I can only say that I am a believer.

Dan Rice

Author's Forward

~

BEFORE ROUTE 66, there was no getting to Southern California for the average traveler, but its creation in 1926 changed all that. Route 66 was also the first paved road across the U.S.—something done during Prohibition to keep Al Capone's booze deliveries flowing from Chicago to St. Louis. By paving the road and guaranteeing his deliveries, regardless of the law, Capone's illegal businesses continued to generate cash flow and thereby coaxed our struggling economy back to health.

In just a few years, the entire 2,448-mile length of Route 66 had been paved from Chicago to L.A., an inconceivable concept in the world at the time because paved roads were expensive. To have one that cut across the entire country and opened up California to everyone was quite a cutting-edge construction project. It quickly became the most famous road in the world, connecting every significant town from Chicago to Los Angeles by the one thing they all now had in common: a Main Street. Towns were connected like a dot-to-dot puzzle, and the phrase "America's Main Street" was born for Route 66. This magnificent road gave us a chance to not only see America for the first time but also to know the character of the people in every American town along the way. Those interactions reminded us of what it meant to be Americans. You could "get your kicks on Route 66," and before long, there was a song and even a TV show about it.

In their fictional travels on Route 66 each week, the characters of Tod and Buz drove their Chevy Corvette across the USA, while meeting and helping people live better lives. As well as helping the fictitious characters in each episode, Tod and Buz also unwittingly saved the Chevy Corvette from being discontinued by GM. In the process of showing the classic American road to the country each week, Route 66 contributed to the popularity of the Corvette, which caught on like wildfire, inextricably linking GM and Route 66 from that point forward. The Corvette soon became an iconic symbol of America in its own right. Route 66 wasn't only exciting, the experience of it, whether in real life, on the radio, or on TV, helped capture the lightning that was the USA in a bottle.

Unfortunately, the feeling of grandness and awe at being an American that Route 66 helped define didn't last for long.

After a visit to Germany, President Eisenhower conceived of a "newer and better" highway system. While there, he'd seen the Autobahn and was completely taken with it. He believed that an interstate system would benefit the U.S., and so the seeds of destruction for Route 66, and all the towns along it, were planted.

The stretches of the new interstate that spanned from Chicago to L.A. were actually built right alongside the existing Route 66, but there was one construction oversight: some sections of the new highway went for miles and miles without an exit to any of the many towns on Route 66. That meant that even though a town might be a stone's throw from the new interstate—literally fifty feet in some cases—there would be no exit and absolutely no way of accessing that town from the new road. If there were no exits to these towns, with no access for the people driving past them, the feeling was that many towns would simply dry up and die.

By the time the interstate was complete, Route 66 was, in fact, sealed off in a lot of areas from the many cars whizzing past on the new highway. People were no longer able to stop at any of the businesses along the way, and with no demand, there was no need for supply. Businesses went under quickly, and many of the little diners, hotels, and mom-and-pop shops in small-town America that helped build this nation to greatness at the height of our productivity slipped away into the annals of history.

The road was officially decommissioned in 1985, just shy of her sixtieth birthday, and the next few years were not kind to 66. For a "Mother Road," it wasn't treated like any mother before her. Moms were to be honored and cherished, and even in the places where you still could access Route 66 and the towns along it, the road became largely forgotten. People had taken to the faster, less scenic interstate, and they had less time for pleasure driving. Skipping past on the interstate, avoiding the people and places on Route 66 that had built this country, seemed like robbing yourself of knowing your own heritage.

My heritage has always mattered a great deal to me, maybe because as a child, just when I thought I'd figured out what it was, it fell apart.

Who I was, what I'd been, and what I'd become seemed in question after the massive changes taking place around me in the USA landscape of the 1970s and '80s. That's because, just like the towns on Route 66, my hometown of Flint, Michigan, was going through a severe tumult. With its identity completely turned upside down and forced into a state of flux, everything and everyone associated with it was also thrown into chaos. Flint was in serious danger of becoming a ghost town compared to the glory days I'd experienced there as a kid, and now I was seeing the same thing happening right across the country. Many ghost towns appeared on Route 66 after my first trip on it across America with my dad in 1985. Each of these forgotten towns on 66 knew the story of Flint's rise and fall because they'd all experienced it themselves with the creation of the federal highway system. Our long-time identity and legacy as Americans was thrown up in the air everywhere. Where we'd all eventually land, no one seemed to know.

In a practical sense, I knew that in an era where time was such a valuable commodity, all these interstates skipping past these truly American towns had their purposes. I traveled on them myself, so I guess I could appreciate that, but I also knew that, as the Japanese car companies had done to the Midwest, these interstates had sucked the water from the roots of this country's greatest Americans along Route 66. Ironically, in making travel easier, the creation of the interstates had contributed to the downfall of our colorful glory years as a nation.

If more exits had been built on the interstates and if someone had just given these towns a chance, they might have been able to grow beyond their past glory into something even more magnificent. It didn't matter to me what kind of ghost towns they'd become because I started to see them for what they'd been and what they could still be, if given the chance.

I began to feel for the people and the families who'd lived in the towns along the route. They'd been proud Americans, like we'd been in Flint, and they'd been happy with the lives they lived. All that was left now of many of these lives were the shells of cars and empty buildings along the road that had once represented those prosperous, happy lives.

Just as the life I'd known in Flint had been taken from all of us when GM pulled up stakes and left us behind, these proud Americans had known what it felt like to have the best of America taken from them.

At that moment of realization, I felt surprisingly aligned with the spirit of Route 66.

One

~

"The Beginning of My End"

AFTER MY ACCIDENT, I lost the ability to read.

The day it happened, I was walking along the sidewalk to my car, heading to my garage with keys in hand, when I suddenly got to thinking about my second car—I had two. One was a really cool classic Corvette with mirrored T-tops and all the Coke bottle curves that come with an old classic like that. The other was a 1988 Buick LeSabre T-Type, built in my hometown of Flint and still running strong at 210,000 miles, easily the most reliable car I've ever owned. It had sentimental value and had been with me all through college and from one side of the country to the other.

That morning I had the keys to my Vette in my hand, but as I was walking up the sidewalk, a voice in my head said, "Why don't you take the other car?" At the time I didn't recognize it, but I got to thinking, "Yeah, why do I need to drive the Vette to the gym? I should take the Buick." I hadn't driven it in a few weeks, and that's never good for a car, so it seemed like a good thing to do. I didn't have the keys on me, but I kept a spare set on the car, so once I got to it, getting in wouldn't be a problem.

Keep in mind, I was about fifteen feet from the Vette at the time with the keys in my hand. My Buick was actually parked up the street and around a corner, so it made absolutely no sense to switch so late in the game. Regardless, I'd been prodded by that still-small voice, and for whatever reason, I responded to it. It's a good thing I did, too.

About ninety seconds later, I was underneath about three tons of steaming metal, protected only by the strength of the Buick's frame around me.

This is where things get a little fuzzy.

Two

~

"Crawling from the Wreckage"

I WAS THE FIRST CAR in line at the light, waiting for it to change to green. An SUV sped up the street toward me and the opposing stoplight, which also would have been red, of course. However, the SUV wasn't slowing down. In fact, if anything, it appeared to be going faster as it approached the light.

At that point, I realized it was going to run the light.

And run it, it did. It plowed straight into a little car in the intersection and spun it around, which shifted the SUV's trajectory a little due to the impact. Yeah, it was still moving, and still moving fast. Only now, it was moving fast toward me, and I was helpless in its path. I remember thinking, "He's going to hit me."

There was no place to go. It was as if time slowed the SUV, and it seemed to take a couple of days to reach me. Everything was running frame-by-frame in my head.

The truth is, it was on top of me in no more than a split second. It smashed the front driver's side of my car head-on, but because of the SUV's higher center of gravity, it went airborne, rocketing up over the hood of my Buick, which now doubled as a launching pad.

It crashed heavily through my windshield, glass exploding through the car's interior. As the impact catapulted my head forward, the SUV's front passenger-side tire came through the windshield and slammed my head backward. That may not have been a problem had the tire not been attached to the SUV, but the fact that the SUV was still attached meant there was a severe amount of momentum behind it. Why it didn't break my neck or take my head clean off, I don't know, but what I do know is that if I'd been driving my Vette, with all its glass windows and mirrored T-tops all around and over me, everything from my neck up would have been scraped clean from the passenger compartment as the SUV plowed on through.

Thank God for old Buicks!

People have suggested that maybe if I'd taken the Corvette, I'd have already been past the intersection and safely on my way to the gym. While their point makes sense initially, it doesn't hold water if you look at the course of events. You'd have to look past the fact that by taking the extra time to grab my Buick, I completely missed having to sit at the first light on the corner. Instead of being red when I got there, that light was already green. Had I been in the Corvette, I'd have gotten there earlier, been caught at that light first, and would've had to wait for it to change before turning. The end result is that once it turned green, I'd have been back on that same timeline down to the next corner. I'd have still caught the second light and been waiting for the SUV to plow into me in the Vette. The difference is that if I'd been in the Corvette, my family would have gotten a call about my decapitation.

In any case, the crash was over and I was still alive. I recall looking at the underside of the vehicle from my driver's seat and the tire resting in front of my face on the steering wheel, three-quarters of the way through my shattered windshield.

The pain in my back and neck was excruciating; sort of like Dick Butkus had come out of retirement to flatten me and brought the rest of the Chicago Bears' line to finish the job.

I remember thinking, "I need to get out of here in case there's a fire."

Surprisingly, my driver's side door opened without a problem. I don't know if I actually fell out of the car or got out, but the next thing I remember is being weakly on my feet on the opposite side of my car. The driver of the SUV—a skinny little guy—jumped down out of his high perch, and I remember seeing him on his cell phone. That stood out to me, and I remember thinking that was maybe why he hadn't been paying attention to the red light. I felt woozy and made my way over to the sidewalk.

I stared back toward my car. Looking back at me and pushed at a ninety-degree angle in the street was the Buick's front end, where, a moment before I'd been hit, the passenger door had been.

I remember Mr. Cell-Phone looking at me but not stopping his conversation, sort of like I was a secondary detail to any damage he might have done to his vehicle. He darted all around, looking at his ride—very impersonal.

He had a girl with him, a blonde, who seemed unhurt. At some point around this time, things went dark, and the next thing I remember is peering up at the sky from the concrete sidewalk. I kept trying to get to my feet, and by now there were witnesses all around telling me to stay down. I was either very shaky or they thought I looked tired and needed a good rest. I obviously didn't look that great to them.

People surrounded me like a football huddle until an ambulance arrived, or maybe it was the police—I don't really know. I just remember being very groggy and that some people were isolating my head and neck by strapping me to a board that was later placed in the back of an ambulance. I remember being scared, but too scared to actually demonstrate with any energy that I was scared.

I remember Mr. Cell-Phone being angry that they were helping me and saying, "Oh, he's saying his neck hurts now?" Not a lot of compassion from Mr. Cell-Phone, I guess.

That's a weird thing, too, because I've always been an extremely kind and forgiving guy. If he'd shown the least amount of concern for me, it would have gone a long way at a moment like that, but I remember him being mad and implying that I was faking being hurt. He seemed to miss the fact that my car was destroyed because his SUV was sitting on top of it. Never once did he ask if I was okay. Never once did he say he was sorry. And that's all I remember about him that day—an angry little guy.

From that point on, I'm not sure what happened; things are a little hazy. I remember the EMTs in the ambulance discussing the first car that had been hit in the intersection. There'd been a mom and daughter in it, and the daughter was going to the hospital with burns on her face. I don't know if that meant their car had caught fire or if an airbag had burned her or what. I just remember feeling sorry for the little girl, hoping she wouldn't be scarred for life or anything. Kids can be cruel, and I'd have hated her to suffer because of someone else's carelessness. Come to think of it, I wonder if Mr. Cell-Phone had gotten mad at her too. He'd been annoyed at me, but she'd had the audacity to let him burn her face!

The next thing I remember is being in the hospital. There was a police officer there who seemed to be having a hard time believing I was the guy in the smashed-up Buick. The way he described it, it had taken a combination of three wreckers working together to get the SUV off my car, and the way the windshield exploded, he couldn't believe my face wasn't sliced into hamburger meat. He was glad to see I was in one piece—I was too.

A patient's rights advocate from the hospital came to me next, and this part is also a little fuzzy. I think he told me I needed to go after Mr. Cell-Phone's auto insurance to pay for my care. He also asked me if I had medical insurance of my own. Ugh … medical insurance.

I told the guy at the hospital I had no insurance, and this was clearly a great thing to do because a miraculous healing immediately took place. They'd x-rayed me, but found nothing broken, so the hospital staff said I could go home. With no insurance, everyone was suddenly content—I was good as new. I said to myself, "I must be okay!" After all, they wouldn't let me leave if there was anything wrong, would they?

So, with no blood pouring down my face and no gray matter squeezing from my ears, they transferred me to the care of a friend, and away I went. No MRIs, no EKGs—no nothing, good to go. They gave me some painkillers, but no umbrella, and sent me out into the rain. I might have been soaking wet, but with those drugs, at least I'd feel no pain. I suppose that's how it was supposed to work.

On the way home, my friend took me to the salvage yard where my car had been taken. I had a lot of stuff in my car, and I thought it best to pull it out of the vehicle before it got any wetter or "relieved" from the car's interior by some salvage yard passerby.

When I got to the yard, the guys there were stunned! Like the cop at the hospital, they couldn't believe I was the guy who'd come out of that Buick. Why was that?

First, the three tow truck drivers had discussed the condition of whoever had been driving my car. It was "clear" to them that the driver of my car would have no face left. The windshield had exploded inward in a way that made it impossible for my face to remain unscathed.

Second, they were pretty sure I had no hands left. The way the SUV had come to rest on my car, the same tire that had smashed into my head had ended up on the dashboard and steering wheel, right where my hands should have been. From the witnesses' descriptions, it happened so fast that the driver—me—wouldn't have had time to pull his hands off the wheel to avoid them being pinned by the tire. So, they were sure my hands were gone. They insisted at least one of them had to be. In retrospect, I guess it's good that I don't always drive with my hands at ten and two.
Pretty soon, even the people in the back of the place, who'd only seen my car towed in, came out to look at me. They couldn't believe it. Again, there were comments that my face "should be gone." I felt lucky. Then again, maybe luck had nothing to do with it. Remember, that voice had encouraged me to take the Buick instead of the Vette. I decided to check out how bad my car was to see what all the talk was about.

After seeing it, I understood. In fact, I'm not sure how I survived, let alone came out of it without a scratch. The windshield had exploded right in front of where my face had been, like a flower coming into bloom. The twisted glass defied gravity, still hanging there like a rose turned on its side. There were millions of shards of glass everywhere throughout the car. They'd sliced the leather seats like a potato cutter slices French fries. How I'd gotten out without a mark anywhere on my body was physically impossible. How I still had a face didn't seem realistic. The only mark on me at all was the telltale red mark on my upper-right forehead from where the tire had hit. It was now numb, and it was soon to shape the course of the rest of my life, though at the time I didn't know that. Everything seemed okay for now, so I got my stuff out of the car and headed home.

About three hours later, I was lying in my bed struggling to stay awake. They tell concussion patients not to go to sleep, but what they don't tell you is that if you have a concussion, all you want to do is sleep. Who on earth was going to stop me from going to sleep though? My girlfriend and I had broken up, and the new girl I'd been dating was out of town. My family was in Michigan, and I was living in California. There was no one around me, no one at all to take care of me.

I WAS MADE IN THE USA. *It was the spring of 1969 in Flint, Michigan, and for the next nine months of my production, God's design team shaped and completed the final assembly for my world debut in early 1970. From all the reports I've heard, my premiere was quite a display. My grandma said that when she first looked at me through the nursery window, I smiled at her. My dad reported that I flipped him the finger. All in all, those two actions probably defined my general response to everything I'd experience in the world better than anything else ever would.*

My mom and dad both worked for General Motors, and when my mom was strong enough to go back to work, she did just that. When I was a toddler, my mom's parents stepped in to take care of me during the weekdays while my parents worked. That meant I spent a lot of time with Grandpa and Grandma Goss, who were young enough to still have their youngest boys at home. This also meant I got to spend a lot of time around Uncle Dave and Uncle Mark, but instead of feeling like they were my uncles, they felt more like much older brothers, and from the youngest age, I was in awe of them. Some of my first memories are of watching them wash their cars while getting ready for dates with whatever cute girl had caught their eye. I remember a '65 teal-blue Impala that Uncle Mark would wax to perfection before jetting off down the road toward his girlfriend's house.

It was the early 1970s, but in my family, it still felt like the '50s or '60s. We were a traditional family with traditional values, and the whole psychedelic drug craze of the '60s had passed us by.

Flint, Michigan, was a wondrous place to be. At the center of so much auto industry activity, it truly felt like you were part of the "heartbeat of America." Everything was squeaky clean and new, and all the greatest restaurants and department stores could be found in Flint. Museums, auditoriums, and concerts with all the biggest acts were the norm in our booming city. It was very much a city ahead of the curve in terms of what it had to offer new arrivals to the area, and magical places like Stepping Stone Falls, with its different-colored lights shining from under waterfalls at night, were beautiful and romantic escapes for couples. Just seventy miles to the south was the even more thrilling excitement of Detroit, the heartbeat of it all, and the motivation for every amazing thing we got to experience in Michigan.

Meanwhile, the very fact that we lived in a state that was home to the largest corporation in the entire world at the very peak of its popularity and fortune was exciting. When the new car models came out, those of us in Flint and Detroit got to see them first. We were treated like family because we'd helped to create them, and it was like belonging to an exclusive club. It almost felt like our own version of Hollywood, because the newest cars were treated to debuts not unlike the biggest and best of the red carpet premieres Tinseltown had to offer. In Flint and Detroit, there were always flashing bulbs and spotlights, big money and three-piece suits. You could feel the energy in the air, and even as a kid, you knew one day you wanted to build cars like your dad did and be in on all the action.

Three

~

"Livin' on a Prayer"

AT THE VERY MINUTE THE SUV careened out of control, the very second that tire came through my windshield and tried to take my head off and for some reason stopping instead of hitting my forehead like a Mack truck, Joe Fish was at that very moment praying for me—praying that Jesus would keep me safe.

You've got to love a guy like Joe Fish: an eighty-year-old ex-Mafio-so I'd met at the neighborhood McDonald's six months earlier.

In line that day was a guy in his mid-thirties, with ripped jeans, leather vest, no shirt at 10 a.m., and he was talking abusively to the woman in front of him. I don't know what it was all about, but he was clearly trying to threaten her out of the line. I looked at my friend George, and he looked at me, and it was clear that the guy was just being a bully. Without even talking about it, I could tell both George and I were in agreement—we needed to say something. Well, we never got the chance.

Out of nowhere, Joe Fish, this eighty-year-old man standing in line behind them started telling the bully to watch his mouth. There were women and children present in the restaurant, and old Joe wasn't having it. The guy mouthed back to Joe, so Joe accused him of being a coward. Joe stated that no real man would pick on a woman. When the leather-clad guy mouthed back again, eighty-year-old Joe calmly "invited" the man to step outside to "talk" about it. The young guy nervously replied, "I'm not scared of you."

To which Joe shot right back, "If you weren't, you wouldn't have to say so. Now, you're gonna apologize to this lady, or you're gonna get beat up by an eighty-year-old man with a wooden leg. Which do you want, buddy?"

Well, Bare-chest got straight to apologizing, and Joe praised him. "Good boy. See how easy that was?" The young guy looked downright sheepish.

Joe then apologized to the customers, some in mid-bite of their Mc-Muffins, hoping he hadn't upset anyone's breakfast. The collective response was that Joe had done a great thing. People thanked him for standing up for what was right, and somebody bought him a coffee. Nearby, Bare-chest looked like he felt about two inches tall and subtly switched his "for here" order to "to go," leaving very soon after.

George and I had to meet the old guy. As it turned out, his real name was Joe Crupi, and he was from New York, but during his old Mafia days, he'd somehow gotten the name Joe "Fish." I didn't ask, and I didn't want to know—I didn't want to upset him or his wooden leg.

Joe really had no one left in his life and had committed himself to a lone pilgrimage, so I started making sure he had at least one person he could count on seeing once a week. From that Saturday on, Joe and I would meet for breakfast at Mickey D's, and he'd tell me how God had empowered him with "the strength of ten men" or how he'd been the original guy to coin the phrase "fuggetaboutit." His face would turn red with frustration as he stated, "I made that up! It's mine! But do I get the credit? No!"

There was always some new, fantastic story about how Joe had impacted the world. "God had me raise a man from the dead the other night! THE DEAD! I got prayer power!" And while some of the stories were wildly unbelievable and others completely hilarious, I'm sure Joe didn't mean to be eliciting so much laughter with them. Still, he knew I was his friend, and he was always absolutely thrilled to share the stories with me and fill me in on what was new in his life each week.

The day of my accident, I didn't meet Joe for breakfast. For some reason, I'd decided I had to skip it that day, and that Joe and I would see each other the next week instead. Considering what happened afterward ... I don't know ... maybe God wasn't too happy with my decision.

As I lay there in my bedroom after the accident, my forehead now increasingly numb from the "Uniroyal" stamp across it, I got a phone call.

It was Joe Fish.

This in itself was significant. Joe had never called me before. He wasn't the richest guy, so he didn't have a phone at home or a cell phone, and it wasn't exactly convenient for him to make phone calls. And while it can be argued that I'd never missed breakfast before either, which had alarmed him, something more powerful had motivated Joe to call.

"Danny?" Joe inquired at the other end of the line.

If they weren't actual blood relatives, nobody called me Danny, but this was Joe Fish, and I didn't think challenging an ex-Mafia guy was in my best interest.

"Hey, Joe."

"Danny, you all right?"

"Uh, yeah ... I guess, Joe."

"Danny, I've had a check in my spirit. Been on my knees all morning for you."

"What do you mean?" I asked.

"Praying! Reaching out to the Living God! I've been praying for you!"

I'm not even sure I responded to this. I just remember asking, "Why?"

Joe continued. "I felt like something was wrong. Like you were in danger. I thought you needed protection, so I didn't go to breakfast. I got on my knees and started asking God to cover you in the blood of His son Jesus! The impenetrable armor of His son's blood ... nothing can penetrate it, Danny! So I been praying for five or six hours ... are you sure nothing happened?"

How could I possibly respond to that?

I filled him in on exactly what in fact had happened. How my head managed to stop an entire SUV ... how I didn't have a mark on me, how the glass was everywhere. I told him all of it.

The voice on the sidewalk, "Why not take the Buick?" rang in my ears. I replayed the way the glass had exploded through the car but left no marks on me, the way that 6,000-pound SUV came to an absolute stop as it hit my 190-pound body. I desperately searched for words.

"Thanks, Joe."

"Hey, Joe Fish loves ya', Danny. And so does Jesus! Remember that!"

I believed him. I had to write this book. And Joe Fish gets all the credit.

Four

~

"Highway Star"

THE NIGHT OF my accident, I actually went to a party and proudly showed people the red spot on my forehead. Other than being sore and having a headache, I thought I was fine, but for all the hope I had that things would be okay, I found out different the day after.

I woke up in the morning and could barely move. From the base of my skull to the bottom of my back, no amount of twisting, moving, or bending could relieve my discomfort. It probably distracted me from the quiet numbness still tingling in my forehead. The only thing I could do was lie on my back on an extremely hard, flat surface. For some reason, that was the only thing that gave me any kind of relief.

I also had a pounding headache accentuated by extreme dizzy spells each time I stood up. Let me just say: Vertigo sucks!

So I lay in bed at home for about three days, tortured by the fact that I couldn't find a comfortable way of lying, and completely unable to do anything about it by standing up. I thought I was going to go mad. It was strange that somehow I found comfort in the numb tingle in my forehead. As the other pain in my neck and back intensified to an excruciating level, the headaches and dizziness made sense, but the tingling felt oddly like life. Something was going on there that didn't hurt, and that was worth something in my mind. In fact, it intrigued me.

Why did that spot tingle? Not ache, but tingle. You know how when your foot or hand has fallen asleep and you get that tingling feeling of the blood rushing back into it? Well, instead of the painful pricking needle sensation that can sometimes accompany that, I'm talking about just before then, when it's still sort of a pleasant tickle. That's just about as close to describing it as I can get. So, in some way, the tingle in my forehead was giving me some enjoyment and some relief from the headaches and pain in my back and neck.

I knew the numb spot couldn't actually be a good thing, but I'd been smacked in the head by a giant tire, so it made sense that I'd feel a little out of the ordinary, right?

I tried not to pay too much attention to it, and while the headaches came and went, the constant pain in my back and neck was impossible to ignore.

I was sick of lying around the house, though. I had to figure out how to deal with these aches and pains, however long they planned on lasting, so I could get out of the house and back to work. Ironically, my back and neck bothered me so badly that it made the "numb head" stuff seem to be the least of my problems.

Boy, was I wrong. The numb head stuff was the tip of the iceberg, but it would be a while before I figured that out.

Five

~

"Don't You Push Me Down"

EVEN THOUGH I HAD a master's degree in psychology, 2002 found me working for Universal Studios, courtesy of a friend. He was an independent producer and needed a writer's assistant, which turned out to be an executive assistant's job. He also threw in the kicker that "if you work as my assistant, I'll show you how to produce." It felt like winning the lottery. I was working in a business I had a passion for, and his writing partner, Billy, was so entertaining that not only was I learning a ton, I was laughing a lot as well. I was very happy.

The drawback was that the job had no healthcare coverage. It turned out that working for an independent production company through Universal Studios wasn't the same as being a direct employee. Still, I had always been extremely healthy, so it didn't seem like much of a risk.

So, after my accident, on November 9, 2002, when I called in to tell my boss, he understood that I was in enough pain to need a few days off.

There I was, smashed in the head, my neck and back wrecked, and I'd been lying flat on my back in my house for three straight days while my forehead tingled. That low-grade headache was growing in intensity, and as it grew, the dizziness seemed to be getting worse . As long as I stayed flat on my back, I felt like it was manageable.

I didn't, however, feel I had the luxury of staying in bed forever. Besides, what good could come from my staying home, waiting for all the discomfort to go away? It wasn't like my job didn't need to be done. They might have to replace me. Anything was possible. Hollywood could be tough, even among friends.

It was no easy journey into the office because I'd developed such bad vertigo following the accident, and the drive in that morning didn't help at all.

Generally, I always got to work before anyone else, and this morning was no different. Usually by the time everyone else rolled in, I'd started our coffee and was answering phones or proofreading scripts or working at the computer on whatever we had going.

However, that particular morning my neck and back were causing me a lot of pain. Once I'd gotten to work and started the morning's coffee, I realized I couldn't keep functioning normally. Since no one else was around, I cleared off one of the desks. I put myself on the hard, wooden surface and was grateful for the feeling of stability underneath me. I'd felt like an accordion standing on end with the top side about to topple to the floor. There was just no stability or strength when I tried to stand up straight. Now that I was on the desk, though, I could rest for a moment.

At about that time, my boss's partner, Billy Brown, walked in.

He took one look at me sprawled across the desk and burst out laughing.

Great impression to make on my first day back, you know? I got caught by the boss literally lying down on the job.

Anyway, Billy was an entertaining sort, more like the clown of the office instead of my other boss, so the fact that he was laughing made me feel good, which was a pleasant alternative to what I'd been feeling moments before. The guy had one of those infectious natures. He made some funny comment along the lines of me looking like a dead deer strapped across the hood of a redneck's truck. I guess a grown man stretched across someone's desk wasn't the first thing he'd expected to see that morning. And I admit, it must have looked completely bizarre. In the midst of his laughter, I think he suddenly deduced that all was not right with my world.

"What happened to you?" he choked through his chuckling.

I figured out that somehow this was the first he'd heard about what had happened to me. Hadn't the fact that I'd been gone for three days made an impression on anyone?

He told me I should go home and get some rest, but given the fact I'd already been doing that for a few days, I tried to be tough.

"Nah, I'm okay. I just need to lie here for a minute."

Billy busted out laughing. "You're not okay! You look bad, man. Really, you should go home."

But I stayed. And of course, that made me fair game for Billy's daily comedy routine. He made the whole situation funny, he really did, and I suspect that somehow he was trying to take the edge off my pain by making me laugh.

Repeatedly throughout the day, as people would arrive, Billy would greet them by telling my story. Invariably, I'd be lying across a desk to give my back some relief or to relieve my dizziness. Each time Billy saw that, he'd get such a kick out of it that he'd find some newly arrived person to tell my story to. Keep in mind that Billy was and continues to be to this day an Emmy-winning master storyteller. I think by the end of the day, he'd enhanced my story so much that the SUV had flipped three times in the air before exploding into a ball of flame on top of me, smashing my car about forty feet into the earth, where I'd been removed by a team of vacationing Kentucky coal miners or something. I mean, it was such a great story that I wished it was true. It was way better than what had actually happened, and it was becoming so grand a tale, what a stud I'd become for surviving! Okay, though, back to reality.

At the end of the day, Billy happened by my desk, and aside from all his joking, he became uncharacteristically serious.

"Hey, I know you're going to want to believe that you're all right and forgive this guy that hit you and all that. But I'm telling you, you're not all right. My wife had an accident not too long ago, and it always turns out people are hurt way worse than they think."

He had a piece of paper in his hand, which he plunked down on my desk.

"This is the number of a lawyer, and he's a really nice guy. His name is Tracy Baer. I want you to call him."

I balked and said I didn't want to sue anybody. Billy didn't respond well to that. He turned his gaze purposely on me, intent on imparting his message.

"Okay, okay, I know … you're a Christian and want to act in certain ways because of that. But take it from an old Jew when I say you've got to be smart about this. You're going to need a lot of help. More than you know right now. Nobody else might tell you this, but I'm telling you. So I'm telling you to call this guy as a condition of your job. If you don't call him, don't come in tomorrow."

This was exactly what I needed to hear. The strength of the message was mixed with concern for my welfare, and I was seriously touched by it. Beyond that, although he'd never commented on it, I think Billy knew how badly I wanted to keep moving forward with my career. He knew that if he appealed to me through my job in a way that also required me to care about myself, he could get me to get the help I needed.

That admonition changed my life.

He left for home, and I called the lawyer, Tracy Baer.

Billy hadn't exaggerated. Tracy was extremely kind, not something I was used to with the lawyers I'd dealt with in the movie business. In fact, when he found out I had no family in California to care for me, he immediately drove out to check on me personally.

By the end of the day, Tracy had me scheduled for an examination of my back and neck—the first of my many, many doctors' appointments to come. He'd taken my case and, to my good blessing, ended up becoming a trusted friend throughout my ordeal.

If I'd known how much darkness I was about to face, I'm not exaggerating when I say I'd have killed myself right there and then. Things were about to get a whole lot worse.

A few weeks after my accident, the numb spot was still there, and I was still in a monstrous amount of pain, but on the good side, I'd found a way to get temporary relief from my back and neck injuries.

Within walking distance of my house was a chiropractic office, and in the hopes of alleviating the pain, I'd started treatment there for my neck and back. The chiropractor gave me some great advice that very first week: "Get back into the gym immediately."

Despite the amount of pain I was in, the fact that I'd broken no bones or torn any muscles or ligaments meant that I should be able to stay in good shape. In fact, it was imperative I did. He also explained that most patients generally wait until their pain subsides before returning to working out. That's counterintuitive to good health and a huge mistake, he said, because by not going to the gym, a person doesn't get stronger. They get weaker, and their problems are compounded by their weakening physical condition. Subsequently, they take longer to make a full recovery—if they recover at all.

I'd been in the gym a lot before my accident, and because I'd been active, even with my back and neck pain, my physical functioning was still more than what the average guy had. I still had most of my capacity for full range of motion.

If I didn't go back to the gym, I'd begin to lose that functioning due to lack of muscle use, and my injuries would start to dictate a decreasing scope of my abilities. The chiropractor was emphatic that I didn't want that. He suggested instead that I continue to do everything I could. If I needed to modify certain things for the time being, I should be free to do that, but I should look at those modifications as simply temporary changes to my regular routine. Furthermore, he encouraged me to do all the things with as much intensity as I could muster, so at least in a physical sense, my body stayed able to do the things it always had. At least physically, then, the aftermath of the accident wouldn't affect me for long. He promised that he'd do all he could in the meantime to ease movement through regular adjustments until I felt okay.

I'd started going to see the chiropractor three times a week, and immediately after seeing him, I'd feel better. He'd adjust me, and I'd feel all these warm endorphins flooding my neck and back joints for the next thirty minutes or so. It was fantastic to get that feeling of relief, no matter how short the duration.

My first brain malfunction occurred about three weeks after the accident.

There I was, thinking I was on the mend. I was back at work, going to chiropractic care, and maintaining my strength in the gym. Then one afternoon, late in the day, Billy asked me to make a copy of a computer disk for him, something I'd done many times before.

Keep in mind that we had a bunch of writers with a lot of scripts on several disks around the office, so rather than print out a full script every time someone finished a draft, we'd often make copies of the script on other disks, then hand off the disks to the appropriate people for reading. On this particular day, Billy asked if I could make a disk copy of a pilot script he'd been working on. That was the only file on the disk and the only thing he needed to copy: one script. It was a simple request, and when he went back to his office, I was more than happy to help him. I grabbed a blank disk and went back to my computer.

What the heck was I supposed to do from there?

I had the disk in my hand. I knew it was supposed to go in the computer, but I had no clue what to do with it beyond that.

I slipped it into the computer, hoping for the best, but nothing happened. Okay, now what? How was I supposed to actually make a copy? I couldn't figure it out.

This was a serious problem. It was a basic duty I did all the time. If I couldn't do this, what business did I have in this job? I started to panic. What was wrong with me? Why couldn't I remember how to do this? I wasn't worried about Billy so much, but in the last few weeks since my accident, my other boss had mentioned a decline in my performance, something he didn't appreciate with us in the midst of trying to save a show we'd put together. This would be more icing on the cake, so I looked at my screen again.

I just sat there. I didn't dare ask anyone else in the office how to do it because I couldn't risk any jokes, sabotage, or gossip that might be spread about me. So I did what would be a common solution for me going forward from that point. I faked it.

I took the blank disk back to Billy, hoping he wouldn't realize that I'd done nothing. This is the thought process of someone who's starting to think irrationally. I mean, how could he not notice there was nothing on the disk?

I left his office feeling like a heel. He'd been nothing but good to me, and here I was being really bad toward him to cover my own incompetence. I went back to my desk and felt like a lowlife. But what could I do? I couldn't remember how to do it, and I didn't want anyone questioning my ability to do my job. Maybe tomorrow, when Billy checked the disk and found it empty, there'd be someone in the building closer to his office who'd end up doing it instead of me. I'd be in the clear, and no one would be any the wiser.

Forty seconds after I left his office, I heard the call. It hadn't worked. Could I try again?

"Sure," I told him.

But I still didn't know what to do!

I got the disk back and returned to my desk. I looked at it and my computer for the longest time. It didn't make sense. I'd done this so many times before, but it was like the information didn't exist in my head. It was as if I'd gone to access a certain file in my own "computer brain," only to find it had been deleted.

One thing was certain. I couldn't mislead Billy about it. Not again.

On the other hand, I didn't want to risk telling him what was going on; it was something I didn't understand and had no answer for. So, like a current of electricity trying to find any outlet for conduction, my survival instincts kicked in and my brain found another solution to making the disk. There's a thing I call the "amygdala remedy." When under periods of undue stress or pain, we humans will look for the easy path to emotional relief from what we're experiencing. Not the best path, just the easiest path. Well, I found one and I took it.

I called my buddy Zach, a computer dude in his own right. He'd have the answer.

When he got on the phone, I felt a little sheepish, but I was more frantic to get the job done than care about how I sounded. As a regular buddy, he'd definitely seen me act like an idiot on lots of occasions, so this time wouldn't be much of a surprise to him.

I told him I'd forgotten how to make a disk, and I could tell from his "Okayyyyy …" that he thought not knowing how to perform such a simple task for someone who worked on a computer all day was kind of odd. He was right. It was a simple exercise. Still, he pushed back his curiosity over why I'd called him for something that someone else in the office could obviously have told me, and he simply walked me through the process.

Making the copy was as simple as this: Zach had me slide the original disk Billy had given me into my computer. At the top left of every computer screen in those days was a task bar with a button labeled as "File." It was common to all computers in 2002, and Zach knew that, so it was easy to walk me through it. I had to click on that "File" button, which, when pressed, automatically unfurls a scroll beneath with a bunch of other buttons, and one of them says "Save as." He had me click on that.

Because Billy's disk was already in my computer, when I clicked "Save as," the name of his file, "Shadow Walkers – Draft," popped up on my screen. Fantastic!

I now had to tell my computer where to save it. How was I supposed to do that?

Zach said there was another designation on my screen that said "Save in." I found it, and it gave a bunch of options of where to save the file. One said I could save it to my "Desktop." I clicked that and saw how it routed the file there. Zach said to click next on the actual "Save" button, yet another designation right in front of my face. For some reason, I just couldn't figure it all out. I clicked "Save," and my computer started buzzing as it routed the file from the disk to my desktop. I was halfway done.

A new icon appeared on my desktop that said "Shadow Walkers – Draft." Zach said it meant the file had been saved there. I could now take Billy's original disk out of my computer. It was no longer needed. The new data on my computer just had to be transferred from my computer's desktop to a new, blank disk.

I grabbed one from the supplies around me. Zach had me insert it where the other one had been.

He had me click on the "Shadow Walkers – Draft" icon on my screen. Suddenly, there it was in front of me, the whole file had opened up. Zach then told me to hit the "File" button at the top of the screen again. I did, and the same scroll unfurled with the "Save as" button, as it had seconds before. This meant that the name "Shadow Walkers – Draft" jumped up again and waited for me to read it in the "Save in" prompt.

This time, instead of saving it to the "Desktop," as I'd done before, Zach told me to save it to the new blank disk I'd just put in the computer. I'd be moving it in reverse, from the desktop to the new disk by choosing one of the other options on my screen, my "Local Disk A" drive, where the physical disk was now sitting.

I clicked the "Save" button and listened to the computer whiz away, moving the information to Billy's new disk. Done.

Zach had walked me through the process, and I was relieved. I told him thanks and hung up.

I just shared that blatantly boring process for a reason: to show the difference between two groups of people reading this right now, and to draw an analogy between the two.

For those of you who are familiar with a computer, you probably just skimmed through the last few paragraphs or thought about going to watch TV out of sheer boredom. Or maybe that "simple process" you've done a thousand times before suddenly reminded you how, before you knew how to do all of this stuff so routinely, it wasn't all that simple initially.

Because of that, for those of you who are completely new to computers, the process probably required close attention, and even then, it may not have seemed that simple.

That's exactly what the relearning process is like for a person with a brain injury. For me, it was the first time I would have to relearn something, but as I was about to repeatedly find, it would become a regular process. Whenever I had to relearn something, I'd have to do it from scratch.

Here's the weirdest part. As Zach walked me through the process, it wasn't like I all of a sudden went, "Oh, yeah! Silly me, how could I have forgotten this?" It wasn't like halfway through the procedure it all started flooding back to me. Quite the opposite, in fact.

It was as if I'd never done it and was hearing the directions for the first time. If he'd stopped telling me anything at any point, I'd have been stuck, with no idea of what to do next. And it's not like there were an excessive amount of steps, really. Just enough that if you'd never done it, you'd be confused.

The directions Zach gave me probably seemed a lot more confusing to both groups than they are in an actual-life application. But if you have no previous experience with whatever your task may be, you now know a smidgeon of the frustration and tedious confusion a brain-injured person faces each time they have to learn or relearn what is essentially a new task.

"Confusion" is the name of your new relearning process, even with something you have visual memory of doing before. If you don't have the recall, however, you might as well be learning it for the first time.

You may be asking yourself, "If you've got visual memory, shouldn't that be enough for someone with a brain injury to remember how to do it?"

No. Here's an analogy: Think of a dream where you did something out of the ordinary for yourself, such as flying a plane. In your dream, you flew it fine. You have memory of it, maybe even of flying it extremely well in the dream. However, when you wake up, do you still have the skills to fly a plane? Unless you're a pilot, the answer is, of course, "No."

Well, why not? You have the visual memory of it, right?

Yes, but you just don't have the recall of the technical skills necessary. Therefore, you can't do it. You cannot fly a plane.

How about this? You might remember hitting a baseball in real life, where visually you can remember seeing the ball fly out into left field. That's one part of the experience, but what technical skills helped get it there?

The technical information that taught you to hold your elbows up, keep your eye on the ball, plant your front foot while twisting your hips and "squishing the bug" with your back foot, then following through with the bat over your shoulder ... these are all part of the technical process that goes into hitting that ball and sending it to the outfield. If you lose the technical skill, you also lose the ability to knock the ball out there.

Therefore, if we go back to the flying analogy, even though you flew in your dreams, you must learn all the technical skills from scratch if you're ever going to do it again in your waking hours. It's the same process for brain-injury patients.

Think of the dream as being analogous to what happened in a person's life before their brain injury. It's stuff you did in the past. The awakened part where you no longer have the skill to do the same exercise is everything that comes after a brain injury. The person's visual memory might be there, but the actual skill that accompanied it is gone and must be learned from scratch.

That's the weird thing about the disk example. It wasn't a dream, and it was the first time I'd experienced the loss of ability to do something I'd done multiple times before. Not only had I copied disks many times in my real "wakeful" life, I had visual memory of doing it before, but for some reason, the recall of actually knowing how to do it just wasn't there.

It's not unlike a light in a room that was once on but is now off. You have a pretty good memory of what was in the room, but with the light off, you can't recall exactly what. The longer the light stays off, the less clear those memories remain.

This is how I felt with this disk-copying exercise. It was completely foreign to me. At the time, I didn't know I was brain-injured, so the whole thing made no sense, and I obviously hadn't thought through the dream analogy yet. For the time being, I shook it off, thinking "whatever," figuring it was a one-time thing, and was relieved to be done with it.

I took Billy's disk to him. He inserted it into his computer as I stood back, anxiously waiting.

"Okay, thanks," he said.

I breathed a sigh of relief. If he'd noticed how stressed out I was by such a simple exercise, he didn't mention it. For sure, he had no clue of what a mental ordeal I'd just been through. But the disk was done, and that was all I cared about at the time.

A short time later, I was at the gym working out with a friend of mine. The point about him being a friend is a big one, because he wasn't just an acquaintance. We'd known each other for a few years, and not only did I know him, I knew his wife, I knew his friends; in fact, several of them were friends we had in common. When I'd worked as a trainer, we'd worked at the same gym. I mean, we knew each other well, and we'd spent a lot of hours together in the gym and elsewhere over the years. He was a very good friend.

You can imagine how weird it was, then, after doing some tricep extensions to look up at him and wonder, "Who is this guy?"

It wasn't like I had no idea at all; it was more like, "I know this guy is my friend, and I know his name, but I have absolutely no idea how I know him." It was all a complete blank.

I remember just staring at him as he talked to me.

It was as if I'd gone deaf. I was so caught up in the surreal nature of the moment that I remember watching his mouth move, but I couldn't hear a word he was saying. I just knew that this loss of information wasn't normal. I knew who he was in name, but I had no hint of how I knew him, how long I'd known him, why I'd known him, or any of the other normal reference points that come with identifying a person.

He looked at me funny for a minute, like maybe he was on to me, so I played it off like I hadn't heard him. He repeated whatever it was he'd been saying, and we went to do some other exercise—he never had a clue.

For the rest of the time that night in the gym, I simply responded to the things he'd say in the way I'd have responded to anyone. I knew the basic fact that he'd been my friend in some way, and therefore, I was unthreatened by anything about the situation. I just knew it was odd that I didn't know how we'd become friends or anything more about him, because clearly I'd known that information before. Hadn't I?

As I left the gym that night, the two of us decided to work out again the next evening. I sat in my car and, oddly enough, as he drove off, I knew who he was again. This didn't make any sense. How could I forget him? I knew who he was! Of course! It seemed impossible to not know!

Clearly, it wasn't impossible. Why I'd blanked on him, I had no idea, but to forget who someone was that I'd known so well didn't sit well. Could this be a result of the numb spot on my head? I wanted to blame it on something other than on myself as a person, and the numb spot was the most convenient culprit. Yes. It had to be the numb spot. Once that went away, I'd be fine, I told myself. I'd just been a little rattled.

Today, I remember that moment as being significant because it was the first time I'd thought there might be something drastically wrong after the accident, aside from my back and neck injuries, and it shook me up.

I was bewildered, so I finally drove home. I avoided my roommates, went to my room, lay down on my bed, and zoned out alone in front of the TV before falling asleep. Little did I know that this solution of isolating myself would become the one of choice for me in the months to come.

With each experience like this, I became emotionally drained, anxious, and paranoid that people would think something was wrong with my head. I didn't want that, but I did hope that things like this would eventually stop happening so I could forget about it all. After all, I felt fine most of the time.

The problem was that I'd feel fine, and then I'd have an episode without any warning. It could be with a person I suddenly didn't know or about something I'd been doing, like the disk copying. Maybe it was a conversation I'd been having and suddenly didn't realize I was in the middle of. I'd just stop talking, leaving the other person wondering why I was such a bad conversationalist. I'd lose grasp of the information I needed to continue. It became a subtle form of torture. I knew I was malfunctioning, I just couldn't determine in what way. It was like my brain was asleep, even though I was fully awake. There were periods when I just had no consciousness of what I was doing.

I remember talking with another friend, Leslie, and I dropped the conversation. I thought we'd just been walking along silently. In fact, I learned later that we'd been talking for about ten minutes, and she'd asked me a question.

I played it off as me being really tired, so she repeated the question. Only I didn't know the context of the question because I couldn't remember any of the conversation leading up to it. My memory retention seemed to be completely gone.

Why was my memory so screwed up? I couldn't figure it out. I'd always had an excellent memory, so to not have one now really worried me. I was always proud of my intellectual abilities, and to suddenly not have them had scary implications.

I started getting really good at playing things off, though. If I forgot someone, I'd wait for a break in the conversation, look them dead in the face, and then, with a completely deadpan expression, say, "Do I know you?" and they'd bust out laughing. The cool thing about it was that if I didn't actually know the person, they'd say "no" and move on. Or they might introduce themselves. With the humor tactic, I kept the people closest to me completely in the dark so they wouldn't look down on me as anything less than I'd been before.

*T*O A KID, *it felt like anyone in Flint could be a breath away from breaking through the ceiling and achieving untold financial riches. And if you worked hard, it was possible. General Motors shared their profits with their employees and made it easy to get ahead and to always be able to afford the newest, coolest cars they were building. The wages and benefits were good, and it was honest work.*

After growing up as a farmer, my dad studied hard and became a skilled tradesman for Buick. By his early twenties, he was quite an impressive guy in his own right, and it was clear to me that the auto business had made that possible, so I grew up loving everything about cars and the industry. I was proud to come from a working-class family, and with the farmland still dominating the Michigan landscape, we had progressed to being a respectable GM family from Flint.

Living in Flint was pretty special back then. You could feel the pulse of the economy. General Motors was the biggest corporation in the world, and between its home bases in Flint and Detroit, we were right in the middle of all the action. As a child, I remember Flint being beautiful, and you didn't have to lock your doors at night. People valued hard work, and they looked out for others who did too. The streets were clean, and it was always easy to find an ice cream man if you wanted a "Good Humor" bar. My memories of Flint are just idyllic.

While my dad worked for Buick, Grandpa Goss worked for AC Spark Plugs. My mom was at Buick with my dad, which is actually where they met. It seemed that everyone worked for the auto industry in some form or another. It didn't matter whether I was with my grandparents during the weeks or with my parents on the weekends, I was surrounded by people who lived and breathed cars.

I couldn't escape the car culture, nor did I want to. Everyone was proud of the identity we had in Michigan. We knew Ford had invented the "horseless carriage" on Michigan soil, and Michiganders were more pleased that GM had come in and expanded the industry to every corner of Michigan's economy. All the car companies were there: Ford, Chevy, Dodge, Chrysler, Pontiac, Oldsmobile, Buick, and even the crème de la crème of fancy cars: Cadillac. There was a car company for anyone who wanted to be in the thick of it, and if you didn't like one brand, you were bound to like one of the others, and even more apt to be driving one of them. It was all you could drive back then. Everything was quality made and built right here in the USA.

Because GM was the world's largest company and all the car companies were based in Michigan, all of their profits around the world came back there. This meant Flint and Detroit were swimming in money, and that was passed on to assembly line workers as well as to the top brass. People weren't wealthy in the flashy way you see in Beverly Hills, but you knew and could feel it was there. The line workers had done the work to build the company by providing the labor, and since the creation of the unions in the 1930s, GM had continued to reward their loyal employees by paying them extremely well. The bottom line was, if you lived anywhere around Flint, you could live well, and we did.

We weren't rich, but we were a solid blue-collar family, although "blue-collar" meant something completely different back then than it does today. If you were blue-collar, you had money and you weren't struggling. People knew you were a dependable, hard worker who'd earned the quality of life you lived through your hard work and effort. That made you extremely desirable and employable in any field because hard workers are tough to find, and someone who's capable of loyalty to their employer is even rarer.

Flint and Detroit were full of workers like this. So much so that many people never did anything to increase their employability beyond the auto industry. They knew they wanted to work for GM or Ford for the rest of their lives, and that's all they ever prepared themselves to do. It was blind devotion.

When Grandpa Goss wasn't at work, it was almost like he was looking forward to going back. I could tell it was only a matter of time until Uncle Dave was working there too. General Motors was like a boy's club, and it seemed an enviable fraternity to be a part of. Mechanical things have always fascinated guys, even guys who have no ability to master them, and to be a part of a company that built things out of steel from the ground up was nothing short of a dream for many people—men and women alike.

I remember when my dad took me to Buick on "Family Day." He took me on a tour that showed me how that finely assembled car began. There was even a foundry where the steel was still in its red-hot, liquid, molten lava stage before it was poured into molds and cooled for car parts. I mean, they did everything from scratch. It was fascinating. How could a kid not want to be a part of that?

In my mom's family, my grandpa worked for AC, Uncle Paul worked for AC, Uncle Dave eventually worked for Chevy, and even Aunt Carol, who was a housewife raising her kids, had a husband, my Uncle Bill, who worked in construction, often at one of the local GM plants. Only Uncle Mark was too young to work for the auto industry, but even he'd grow up to give it a shot when he was old enough to apply.

At the end of the day, our family wasn't any different from the majority of families there. We all held the same belief: working for an American car company wasn't just a job, it was a way of life, and for many, a proud heritage.

Made in the USA. In Flint, Michigan.

Six

~

"Half a Man"

IN THOSE LONG WEEKS after the accident, another thing started happening pretty regularly, and it was kind of lIY(TGL GHHhje320000.

Did you get that?

No? That's because it didn't make any sense, and that's exactly what would happen to me when listening to someone. They'd be talking along, and all of a sudden, none of their words would be coherent. It was as if they were speaking a foreign language because I couldn't make heads or tails of anything coming out of their mouths. There was sound but no meaning to me. In psychology, it's called "aphasia."

I quickly learned that if I didn't understand or even if I did understand but had simply lost the content of the conversation, if I just kept good eye contact with a person, nodded and said "hmmm" or "yeah" every once in a while, people would talk on for days without realizing there was even a problem.

I realized that in most conversations, people aren't looking for feedback as much as they want someone to listen or to bounce ideas off of. People just want to feel heard.

I started having a few cool insights like that. Freed from focusing on the content of conversations and more on the one-sided quantity of words a person will share if uninterrupted, I was able to see that people are fairly lonely, they want to feel valued and hope someone will stick by them and listen in a loyal manner. It started making sense to me why people love their pets so much. Though there is much more to it, obviously, pets are the perfect one-sided soundboards—with an occasional lick of your face for added support.

I was also able to experience something that I'm sure is a basic learning tool in children, something I call "infant-processing." From a therapist's perspective, the phrase "processing" means to not listen so much to what a person says as to how they actually say it. What does their body language tell you? What's the tone of their voice? Are their eyes full of life or are they dull, as if glassed over and bored? Are their muscles tensed or relaxed as they deliver a message? Are they breathing hard or easy, fast or slow? Are they speaking loudly or softly? I imagined before understanding speech that children probably used these same indicators to determine whether a person was a threat or someone safe. Now I was like a baby, without a consistent ability to understand English or know when a person was safe or not. At times when comprehension left me, I'd pay attention to people's "processes," or the way they spoke to me instead. Those clues told me a lot about their "safety factor." Even if I couldn't understand the actual words, their tone guided my emotional responses. If a person acted upset, I'd act upset with them. If they were happy, I'd smile too. People couldn't tell I was clueless.

Interestingly, I started determining a person's general truthfulness from the unspoken messages they put out. I'd watch people smile at me with tightly clenched jaws or while their eyes went flat. When their hostile or tense body language, cold eyes, or breathing did not match their nice, kind words, I'd know they didn't mean the words they were saying. For reasons I didn't know—but still using in the "safe versus unsafe" infant test—I'd decide that contradictory people were either hiding something or couldn't be completely trusted. They were unsafe. I'd get away from them as quickly as possible.

To get an idea of what I mean, think of a time when you asked if someone was upset and they snapped back, "No!" Especially then, you knew the answer was "Yes." You could remove the content of the word completely and know the true answer to your question from the tone of their voice. Now if you added a smile to that person's face as they snapped in that same tone, you'd know something was even more wrong because they were trying to confuse or deceive you with their interactions. It would also give you an opportunity to skedaddle accordingly. That's what I call infant-processing. Determination of "safe" versus "unsafe." Honesty or deception. It was fascinating.

Most often, it wasn't the "safe versus unsafe" or "speaking Greek" scenarios I faced, it was simply losing the thread of a conversation, like I'd done with Leslie. In those moments, I faced a certain danger, which was being put in the awkward situation of being asked for feedback. When you don't understand all of what's being said, that becomes pretty tough to give. To keep people off my trail, I figured out a pat response:

"I don't really know."

They'd usually just continue on, then, or laugh, or something, but the bottom line is, they couldn't tell there was anything wrong with me, and that's what I needed. The last thing I wanted was for people to think I was crazy, or retarded, or anything other than what I'd always been.

Sometimes in a conversation, I'd use an old therapy technique I'd learned from my grad school mentor in San Diego. As a therapist, it's really important that people arrive at their own answers instead of getting steered by a therapist, although some people mistakenly believe a therapist is supposed to give advice. My mentor would say to me that if his clients asked what he thought about something, he'd ask them why it mattered what he thought. And he wouldn't be smarmy about it but genuinely interested in why it mattered so much what someone else's thoughts were. That was a therapeutic tool for getting to the root of why they needed reassurance from outside sources, and it usually led to really good insights for him and his clients.

If I got lost in a conversation and someone wanted my opinion, I'd slide out of it by just providing good therapy. Other than their processing, I wouldn't comprehend anything they'd said, but if they asked me for feedback, I'd ask slowly, in a very measured tone ...

"Why are my thoughts important?" or "Does it really matter what I think?" or the killer, "Doesn't it matter more what you think about it?"

If they pressed, I'd follow up with "I don't think it matters what my thoughts are," or I'd juxtapose any of those with "I don't really know how to respond to that," and I could get out of answering questions in almost any conversation.

Ironically enough, people would think I was such a good listener! The truth is, I hadn't understood a thing they'd said!

If only I'd known this secret before I shelled out all that money for therapeutic training in grad school!

More to the point, the only thing not muddled in my head, unlike all the conversations and words flying around me, was that things weren't getting better for me, and I didn't know what to do about it.

I'd gone to grad school to study the psychology field, human behavior, marriage and family therapy, the brain, all of it. And yet, after all that, I'd never heard of anyone who suffered with anything even remotely resembling the kinds of things I was dealing with. I hadn't worked in neuropsychology. I didn't know about the Brain Injury Association of America. I'd worked with psychiatric patients who had all kinds of brain maladies, things like schizophrenia, delusional disorders ... you name it. Still, I'd never seen anyone whose symptoms resembled my own. What the heck was I dealing with? Who was I becoming? How could I get my normal life back?

I had no idea what to do. As far as brain injury was concerned, the thought was starting to cross my mind. My numb spot was, after all, still there, although its sensation was gradually turning more "dull and fuzzy" than "tingly." It just didn't have the sharpness it originally had, but make no mistake, it was there.

I wondered more than ever what the spot meant. Had I been brain-injured?

I had no way of diagnosing myself. Even with a master's degree and part of my doctoral work out of the way, I didn't know much about neuropsychology or brain injury. Other than a physiological psych course I'd had years ago, my specific field of discipline wasn't especially focused on the actual mechanical workings of the brain.

The understanding at the time was that if you were brain-injured, you were brain-injured. It wasn't like an arm or leg that healed after being broken. You only had one brain, and the conventional wisdom was that it didn't repair itself. The last thing I wanted to admit then was that I actually was brain-damaged if there was no hope of recovery for me.

This cloud of confusion was going to be my new life? No way. I wouldn't accept that. So instead, I just kept hoping things would get better.

They didn't.

Seven

~

"Everything Put Together Falls Apart"

T HE LAST WEEK OF JANUARY, three months after my accident, my boss called me to his office. His first words? "We need to talk."

These are always the last words you want to hear, whether they come from a boss, your girlfriend, spouse, significant other, or God Himself because you know that hearing them is not a good sign.

The bottom line with my boss?

You know the story. I wasn't "cutting the mustard," "working out," "pulling my weight," pick whatever euphemism you like best. Anyhow, he'd already hired my replacement, so I didn't have much to say about it. It was one of his daughter's friends. The kicker was that my last day would be in a week, February 7 ... my birthday.

Happy Freaking Birthday ... You're unemployed!

I knew things weren't right with me. I knew I didn't have it completely together anymore, and this would be an impossible situation if it meant stepping into a new job and performing well. I figured that with how scattered I was becoming, I'd probably get fired right out of the gate at any new job I managed to get. At least working in a place where I had friends, I'd had a safety net, so to speak, to catch me while I was struggling.

It didn't matter now. I was out.

I started to realize how alone I was. I felt reviled by everyone around me to the point of paranoia.

More than that, to me, the pink slip meant I was a failure. Everything leading up to this job and to this moment had meant nothing because, in the shape I was in, I was in no condition to go forward anywhere else.

There would be no producing career. Nothing. I was at a loss.

Before I left, Billy, good guy that he was, told me that he didn't have anything to do with me being let go. He couldn't really stop it because he hadn't hired me in the first place, his partner had, but he seemed genuinely sorry and concerned and hopeful that things would work out for me. He told me if I needed anything, to keep his home number and I could be sure to call on him or his wife.

That was a huge overture, and I left feeling like I at least had some base of support I could touch down with if I needed it. That's huge in the life of a brain-injury patient—knowing you have support is critical.

In the years since I left, Billy and I have remained friends, and he's told me that he knew when I left that day that I wasn't the same guy I was before my accident, and he also knew I was going through a lot mentally.

In hindsight, it's not easy to be too upset with my other boss. While I thought I was holding my job down decently, Billy remembers times that were a little less than stellar. At times, I'd be at my desk staring off into space for long periods. He also said I complained about constant headaches a lot. I have no memory of talking about headaches, but I don't doubt it. I do recall the headaches and a lot of dizziness, I just don't have any memory of talking about them. As for the episodes of staring off into space, it's almost as if I lost time in those instances because I don't remember any of that at all.

That's the thing, though. A brain-injured person doesn't always know the extent of what they're dealing with. All we know is what we're conscious of. If my brain suddenly decided to retreat somewhere while trying to heal itself, it'd leave me there blank and staring off into space, only I'd have no idea about what was happening.

I probably didn't even realize I'd had a break in the action. No one said they saw anything wrong, and what I did know was wrong with me, I wasn't trying to share. In my head, I was keeping the bad stuff covered and the other stuff of my life together as much as possible.

But Billy was right; I'd been having headaches. In fact, they were getting more and more frequent, and they'd take the steam right out of me, sending me back to my favorite retreat spot at home—bed.

At least in bed I could rest away from the world and wait for it all to pass.

With no job, I didn't really have anyplace else to go. I had no money, so I wasn't out spending any. I just needed, in my own head, to take the time to sleep this situation off. I barely had the energy to make calls to other production companies looking for work.

As my paranoia grew, I told myself they wouldn't want me, and I convinced myself they'd see something was wrong with me. It was this whole negative self-fulfilling prophecy, and, ultimately, I was right. I couldn't find another job. Whatever the reason, something always blocked me, and I'd wind up frustrated. At this point, I started slipping into a depression.

Back to bed I'd go. If I could just get my mind off of my situation, maybe I could think clearly enough to get out there and do it right next time. The problem was that I had so little energy that once I got out there, the smallest block or rejection would amp up my frustration enough to drop me back down in a heap on my bed. It became a real feeding cycle. I didn't feel like I could accomplish anything. My bed, darkness, and my TV became my best friends. I didn't have any leads, and things seemed to be quickly closing in.

I couldn't even rest well. Call it a mix of anxiety combined with headaches and dizziness, but sleep started to get less and less predictable. With the overall chemical imbalances taking place in my brain, it eventually became impossible. I'd stay awake for two or three days at a time, and although I was exhausted, I just couldn't fall asleep. It was as if my body just wouldn't let me.

Other times, I'd be in the middle of doing something, and the next thing I knew, I'd be waking up and a couple of hours had passed. Maybe even a whole day.

Things were getting really bad.

The one thing I did start doing was playing videogames. I'd never really played them much before, but at the time, I lived with two roommates—friends really—and it was getting difficult to cover what I was going through or to rationalize why I'd be up watching TV all night long. Videogames allowed me to explain away my behavior by citing my interest in finishing a certain game. This was made all the easier by the fact that one of my roommates also loved playing them, so instead of keeping him awake while playing, he'd keep himself awake by hanging in there with me. Now my own abnormal sleep patterns wouldn't stand out at all, and that's just how I wanted it.

I hadn't been able to maintain my relationships at work, but since I'd been let go, I convinced myself that at least at home I was keeping my difficulties invisible.

I don't know why, exactly, but sometime during the following spring, I started telling Tracy Baer, Billy's former lawyer (and now mine) what was happening with me.

I'd been paranoid about it with everyone else, but Tracy was the only one who'd been with me all along, so I wasn't afraid to tell him the same stuff I was petrified to tell others. I don't think I'd meant to get into it with anyone, really, but I'd talked with Tracy enough that it was probably what I wasn't saying that got him asking questions.

He was astute enough to fill in the blanks, and that most likely tipped him off to some potential problems. Since I was so paranoid about anyone knowing what I was dealing with, when he questioned me about those very specific things, I don't know why I trusted him, but I did. With no family around, the fact that he'd always acted more like a friend than a lawyer had gone a long way.

For my back and neck problems, he put me in the care of some good doctors, and when I had complaints about any bad doctors, he was always looking out for me and trying to find someone better. Regardless, there was something about him that always said, "I'm your friend and you can trust me," and even with only half my wits about me, I had the good sense to know it.

When I told him some of the weird things that were happening with my head—the things with my memory, my sleep and so on—I remember the look of concern on his face. While he didn't really have any answers for me, he didn't shy away from trying to find them, either.

He set up an appointment for me with a neurologist by the end of the day. I was a little nervous about this because I didn't want to be diagnosed as crazy. Regardless of my own thoughts, however, Tracy explained that I needed to face my problem, so if something was wrong, I could go about getting help.

I finally relented. As long as Tracy was the only person to know, I guessed it would be okay. I just didn't want people to look down on me, pity me, or make fun of me.

A few days later, I showed up for my appointment with the neurologist, a Middle Eastern man in the mid-Wilshire district of L.A.

For those of you who don't know, a neurologist is a medical doctor that specializes in brain functions. Well, whatever this doctor's name, the guy was a total washout at his job, not to mention that I felt like a fast-food meal being quickly assembly-lined through some sort of five-minute medical exam.

He tapped my knee with a hammer, looked in my ears, and did all the things included in a routine physical. Then he took out a tuning fork and made it hum around my ears. He asked me if I could remember a couple of objects. I don't remember what they were now, but when I was unable to recall them for him, he was quick to rush to a verdict. Yes, yes, he was sure he could treat me.

Treat me for what? He hadn't even diagnosed me. What was I getting treatment for? I was still trying to avoid admitting to myself that there was a problem. Was I supposed to accept open-ended treatment for something I hadn't even been diagnosed with?

I may have been nuts at the time, but it seemed to me like the guy sensed a steady amount of cash flowing from my pocket into his, simply because this appeared to be a long-term case. Was he trying to rip off me, the system, or both? Was I just more paranoid, a common condition of someone who's suffered a brain injury? It may have been all of the above, but I didn't know any of that for sure at the time.

As I sat there with him in his office, I began to grow angry. Exceptionally angry. Unlike me angry. I started yelling and baring my teeth, questioning whether he thought he found a sucker in me. This was not like me at all, but I didn't seem able to control it. I demanded a diagnosis from him, and when he didn't give one, I insulted his ethnicity and accused him of being in al Qaeda. I became extremely aggressive, matching his prescription for ongoing care with his ethnicity and accusing him of mental terrorism against me. I made what could have been a sensible conversation into something completely illogical.

I'd never attacked anyone because of their race. In fact, I'd always been the opposite of that, enjoying cultural diversities and encouraging harmony between people. For me to start spewing racist talk at someone was completely out of left field. I'm sure there are those who'd argue it was always in me and that I'm "really like that," but they'd be wrong. This was simply another attack on me by a brain that had too little control and too much access to an open mouth. Regardless, I stomped out of the office calling him "a quack" and vowing never to return. I'm sure he breathed a sigh of relief at that.

That's another problem with brain injuries; you can never really trust whether or not your thoughts are on target because even if there is truth to your view of a situation, your perceptions are so clouded by the injury that it's impossible to tell what's accurate and what isn't. Sometimes you're still spot on, but other times you're just completely out to lunch. Betting on which is right is never a safe bet.

Y OU COULD FEEL *the dignity in Grandpa Goss toward what he did and where he worked. He was a larger-than-life character in my world, and the energy he generated was contagious. He showed me what my life could be like when I grew up. I could have a family. I'd have a job. I'd have friends who were like-minded, and of course, I'd have a little time saved for fun. Part of my grandpa's daily regimen was going off to the Slenderform Health Spa to get in a quick workout, and I used to marvel at how powerful and strong he was. This was, of course, in the days before physical fitness swept the nation, but in a time and place like Flint in the 1970s, where paying your bills wasn't a problem and providing for your family wasn't a struggle, the little bonus things like maintaining your health became available to us before they caught the attention of the rest of the nation. It was a truly progressive time and place to be an American.*

Uncle Dave always sort of marveled at Grandpa Goss, and I was affected by how close they were. As father and son, they were always together, and I was always with them. From the youngest age, I was tossed into the backseat of the car to ride along on whatever errand they'd run together around Flint, and it was always fun. This was in the politically incorrect days before kids had to be in car seats, so often I was just sort of tossed in on my back like a sack of potatoes to gaze up at the sky while sliding around on the vinyl seats and falling onto the floor mats. These are some of my earliest memories, and whenever I was with my grandpa, they involved listening to news radio, which was his favorite. We'd drive around looking at or buying cars that he'd tune up, fix up, and sell. It was magical, and all my memories of that time are quite spectacular.

On my dad's side of the family, things were a little different. Dad came from a family of farmers and had grown up on a farm west of Lansing, Michigan. He still had that same strong work ethic that all farmers have, which is basically to be up early in the morning and off to work without a complaint or a bad word. There was work that needed to be done, and he'd learned early on to simply get on and do it. Anything else was simply a waste of time and delayed finishing the work, which was always the goal before earning the right to enjoy your day. If you could figure out a way to enjoy the day in the midst of your work, then you'd truly stumbled on a secret that could make your whole life wonderful.

Around the same time my dad left home to work for GM, his broth-

er Larry did, too. Uncle Larry worked for Oldsmobile in Lansing, and, like my dad, he was tough and farm-honed through and through.

My dad's parents, Grandpa and Grandma Rice, were also farmers, although Grandma probably had her sights set well past the wheat field horizon long before they left the farm. She encouraged my grandpa to finish his degree, and, while raising two boys, he managed to graduate. In 1961, my grandpa finished his stint as a farmer and went to work for the federal government, while my dad and Uncle Larry ran the farm. By the early 1970s, Grandpa had done a good enough job for the government that he was promoted to a position at the Department of Labor in Chicago, Illinois, and with both of their boys now grown and married, off to the big city they went.

My dad's parents were always sort of a celebrity couple to me. While George Jefferson was a fictional character on TV who'd fought his way up the social ladder, my grandparents were real. They'd started out poor, worked hard, and in the end, literally lived in that high-rise condo in the sky.

I didn't see them often, but when I did, it was always a celebrated event.

Meanwhile, in Michigan, I continued to spend time at Grandpa and Grandma Goss's house surrounded by the love of my family. I loved it there so much that when my parents came to pick me up for the weekends, I cried and cried because I didn't want to leave my grandma and grandpa. My dad was concerned I didn't really know where I belonged, but with my mom still working, I felt like my grandparents' place was home.

It wasn't long before my mom left her job at Buick and came home to be a full-time housewife and mom. This was still a pretty common job for women, and in that era, it was still an extremely respected thing to do when you had kids. After all, we weren't all that far out of the Beaver Cleaver era, and even today, I think it's one of two of the most important jobs in the world. The only other job to rival it is being a father, and fortunately for me, I had a good one and no shortage of other takers if I ever needed them.

My parents and I moved to a small town in mid-Michigan just fifteen or so miles north of Flint. Surrounded again by farmland, I'm sure my dad felt comfortable there, and I had the chance to experience the peace and tranquility of the rolling countryside during the day mixed with the sounds of crickets and bullfrogs in the dark, starry nights. It was idyllic.

One of the treats I used to really love, and one of the things that helped me maintain that feeling of connection to Grandpa and Grandma Goss, were the sights and sounds of the many trains that came through the country in our small town. My mom was always at the grocery store to pick up something for that night or the next night's dinner, and the rails ran just past it. I'd marvel at how close we'd get to the big trains in our car as we waited for it to cross through town. They seemed so powerful, and their whistles were all so wonderfully different. The engineers always impressed me as the engine plowed through our town, followed by the long display of colorful train cars that proved how strong the engine was to pull them all. At the end of every train was a bright red caboose, and in the top of the caboose there'd always be a man hanging out the window who would kindly wave back at me as the train went on out of town on its mysterious journey to somewhere.

I'd ask my mom where the train was going and learn that the same rail line passed just a half mile from Grandpa and Grandma Goss's house. It was almost as if by waving at the men on the trains, they could wave at my grandpa and grandma for me, and that made me feel somehow closer to them. Every train's trek through town was a comforting connection to the grandparents I'd loved and left behind in Flint.

Not that I'd left them behind permanently when I'd moved back full-time with my parents—heck, no. My mom and my grandma were extremely close, and I was still down there to visit them nearly every day. The only real difference was that I didn't sleep there as much, but the days that blended endlessly into the next with my grandpa or Uncle Dave and Uncle Mark were largely over, and even at that young age, I longed for "the good old days" of life at their house.

Anyhow, every train passing through our town and the sound of their whistles at our home a few miles away were comforting reminders that my grandpa and grandma weren't far away, and it showed a little boy that the world wasn't as big as it sometimes felt.

I learned to love trains from those experiences. They went everywhere. I even learned that they went to Chicago, where Grandpa and Grandma Rice were, and when we went to Chicago to visit them, I'd always be amazed by the gigantic rail yards we'd see along the way. It was such a dream existence in Chicago, so far removed from the small-town life I was growing up in. I had no concept of what their big-city "jet-set" life was like, but when my parents and I went to visit, just in the scope of its sheer expansiveness, Chicago left Flint in the dust. From my grandparents' condo high in the John Hancock Building, the city seemed to go on forever. It was just so much more glamorous than Flint; something I didn't even know was possible because in those days, Flint was still a magnificent place.

Eight

~

"Work Me, Lord"

AFTER MY EXPERIENCE with the first doctor, the good Mr. Baer started talking about a different doctor he knew over at UCLA Medical. His name was Dr. Barry Ludwig. Tracy was certain Dr. Ludwig could get to the bottom of what was going on with me. He said he was willing to send me there if I wanted, but he also wanted me to know that Dr. Ludwig was probably going to be a little more expensive.

I didn't care. I wanted help with this. If there was someone who could fix me, I needed to see him before I completely tripped out.

As soon as I met Dr. Ludwig, I had a good feeling about him. I don't remember everything we talked about, but I remember he did quite a bit more than the first guy did. He sat down with me.

He talked to me.

He was interested in me.

He used the tuning fork, but he also had me looking at his fingers, tracking movement, answering lots of questions, just a bunch of things that hadn't been covered in the first doctor's assessment. And by the end of that first meeting, he made a statement that seemed like a blessing and a curse.

"You have what's called 'post-concussive disorder.'"

Some people call it "post-concussive syndrome." Either way, he told me that it generally accompanies a head trauma and that it can last over a period of six months or so. Most important, he said a post-concussive disorder included all the symptoms I'd been experiencing. That was encouraging. I knew what I was dealing with. A "post-concussive disorder."

Just knowing the name gave me back a sense of control over my life. Even better was the fact that almost six months had passed since the accident, so according to Dr. Ludwig's description, could I possibly be at the end of all these rapidly developing and emerging inconveniences in my life?

Well, for me, the answer turned out to be "no," but at least on that day, the diagnosis gave me some hope.

The other thing Dr. Ludwig did that day was write a few prescriptions for some different medications. Painkillers, sleep aids, antianxiety medications, and antidepressants. It was a whole host of drugs designed to combat what I was dealing with. I didn't want to take them, and I told him so, but just like Tracy, he gently redirected me.

"You don't have to look at these as a permanent solution. We can get you other help. But your brain chemicals are out of balance right now, and these will settle you for the time being. We'll start you on some samples. You'll take them for a few weeks, and then let me know how you're doing. Okay?"

The last thing Dr. Ludwig did for me that first day was talk about rehabilitation facilities.

What did I need rehabilitation for? It seemed a bit extreme to have me go sit with a bunch of people who I imagined had parts of their brains removed. I'd seen One Flew Over the Cuckoo's Nest! I wasn't like those patients. The last thing I wanted anyone to think was that I was retarded or would need the same types of services as people like that.

There were two different facilities whose names were scrawled on a piece of paper, but I told myself that I didn't need rehab from either of them. After all, since my six months of "post-concussive disorder" were pretty much up, it just figured that soon I'd start to get better on my own.

Shoving the doctor's recommendations away in a drawer, and, despite the obvious fact that I was already ignoring his suggestions for prescriptions and rehab, the thought that my situation could clear up soon made me really happy for the first time in quite a while. I was curious, though.

If my situation could be over so soon, why would rehab even be a consideration? Was there something he wasn't telling me? Was my situation even more serious than he'd let on? No, I didn't believe that. He seemed honest and trustworthy. Besides, if my brain healed and I was back to normal, while his suggestions might be helpful, wouldn't rehab actually be a little unnecessary? No, I definitely didn't want to go to a place like that. Beyond that, a few hours after I'd left his office, my adverse reaction to getting the prescriptions filled became even stronger. No way was I going to put myself in a situation that made me look like a psychiatric patient. I'd worked with those people before I'd made the switch from the psych field to Hollywood, and I was nothing like them! Or so I thought. I told myself I was okay, and I'd keep going until my "post-concussive disorder" was over and life was back to normal.

Despite my background, I now found myself on the "other side" of things. I'd worked in hospitals, private practice, and residential treatment centers where the patients took certain drugs to become regulated and balanced. The thought that I was one of those patients now wasn't something I was interested in even entertaining. When I worked with them, I enjoyed helping people get stabilized so they could live good, productive lives, but they needed the help. I told myself Dr. Ludwig was just being overly cautious. I wasn't like them. I didn't need the drugs.

Unfortunately, I never realized until much later that resisting the medications that day really meant that somewhere deep down, all those years earlier, I'd really been looking down on those people I'd helped. I'd had the thought that because they needed drugs to live normal lives, they weren't really normal. I suppose I'd looked down on them because I thought I was better. Somehow, I guess I'd always seen them as inferior.

It was only fair, then, that I'd now be forced into the ironical situation of having to live with the same judgment from others that I'd put on my own patients and clients, not to mention anyone else in the world that needed medication to get or keep their lives on track. But that was just it. Taking these medications meant I needed to admit that my life was no longer on track—it meant admitting I needed help.

As crazy as it sounds, I still didn't want to admit that, not even to myself.

I kept wanting this to be a temporary thing, not a permanent one, and if I took the meds, I'd never undo the fact that at a certain point in my life, I'd had to take drugs just to get to "normal." Something about those drugs made it a "more-than-temporary" condition to me because drugs would become a permanent part of my history. The fact that taking them was something Dr. Ludwig thought I needed carried with it the implication I wasn't normal.

This was suddenly a huge problem for me because in the small amount of time I'd spent with him, I trusted Dr. Ludwig. That meant I also needed to trust his opinion that I wasn't normal. And if I didn't want to trust that, it meant throwing out his diagnosis of post-concussive disorder, which didn't make sense because all the symptoms he'd listed for it fit me to a tee. He was clearly right—I wasn't normal.

Maybe the more far-reaching implications of my long-term prognosis of "normalcy" were bothering me as well. I mean, after all, if I admitted I wasn't normal now, that could be the first step toward admitting I'd never be normal again, and that would mean this wasn't a temporary situation, that it really was permanent.

Ultimately, the whole decision to take meds forced me to face the ultimate question of whether this confusion and all my other daily mental struggles were going to be a permanent part of my life. Maybe the rehab was a good preventive strategy. I just didn't want all of these weird experiences to become a regular part of my life.

But what if they did become regular?

I had to keep focused on this condition being temporary. Even then, what if I started taking these drugs and found that I actually was a better person on them? Wouldn't that mean that my life had devolved from the point of being a psychological practitioner and so-called expert to now being a lowly, average psychiatric patient?

In my head, that meant one thing: I could never be taken seriously as a practitioner of psychological health because I could only be psychologically healthy with artificial methods, not by any means of my own. That meant my entire college education was a waste. If it was useless to help me, how could it ever be useful to help others? I was obsolete.

Why couldn't I just have studied business like the rest of the kids?

Nine

~

SLEEP WASN'T A CONSISTENT OCCURANCE, but when I did sleep, I'd have bizarre dream experiences.

In the dream, I'd be talking with someone, and I'd lose the thread of the conversation in the same manner as when I was awake. The difference was that in my dream I was conscious that I'd lost the information, and I'd try desperately to remember what I'd been talking about. The variation might be that the person I was talking to suddenly wouldn't have a face. I lost the information of who they were and would try to remember. Sometimes I'd know who they were and would try to re-picture and position their face back on their head, or maybe I'd lose who I'd been talking with completely.

Either way, there was missing information, and as soon as it escaped, I'd try to backtrack my thoughts to retrieve it. The harder I tried to recall the information, the less I was able to do so, to the point where I'd lose the connection to what I was even trying to remember—a person, a place, a thing? It was as if I were being punished for trying to get back the missing knowledge, and now I'd be penalized even further by losing more of my memory, until I had nothing.

It was similar to being slammed into an enclosed gray cinderblock prison with no visual cues to where I'd just been, what I'd been involved in, or who I'd been involved with. I'd try to mentally break free from the cinderblock walls, back to the colorful world I'd just come from, but the harder I tried to break free, the more the walls closed in, until I had a sensation of being trapped in the blankness of my own mind. I felt I was dissolving into the nothingness of gray all around me or, worse yet, being crushed by the walls as they absorbed me. I'd start to have an attack of claustrophobia that would jar me out of my sleep in a full-fledged panic.

I'd leap out of my bed or onto my bed and grab my head, screaming like I'd been robbed of not just where I was, but who I was ... I didn't have any connection to what I'd been thinking split seconds before, and I'd have no connection to where I was waking up either, and that would panic me even more.

Who was I? Where was I? I wouldn't even know what state I was in, let alone the city ... was this Michigan, where I'd grown up? San Diego, where I'd gone to grad school? It certainly didn't look like anything familiar.

I'd whirl around and gape out the window. There was the Universal Studios sign on the small mountain in the distance.

I was in California. I was Dan Rice. I'd worked on that studio lot. What season was it?

That would set me off again, because in California the seasons generally all look the same. There was no frame of reference for the time of year. With nothing to anchor myself to the world around me, I'd find myself in an out-of-control, spiraling, mental freefall where I was unable to get my bearings.

I'd eventually get my breathing under control, but I'd be so awake that going back to sleep seemed impossible. I'd lie there for two or three hours, afraid to sleep for the fear of it happening again. Once I'd found myself, I didn't want to get lost again, and the possibility that I'd one day lose myself forever was horrifying! No, if I stayed awake, at least I could hold onto myself for now.

Eventually, all this thinking would exhaust me and I'd fall asleep again. Those were the good nights.

As time went on, the attacks happened with increasing regularity. So much so that I recognized what I was experiencing and knew I'd probably recover. Strangely, that bit of knowledge was enough to decrease my anxiety a little.

Occasionally, though, I'd do something that would throw a wrench into my routine and really send me for a loop.

My good friend Jay and his fiancée Christy were getting married. Jay said he needed someone to watch his house, so instead of going to Georgia for the wedding, which was extremely cost prohibitive for me at the time, I volunteered to stay at his house and look after Christy's cat.

Picture this. I'd wake up in my own home in the midst a panic attack and not recognize things in my own room. Now I was going to try to stay in someone else's house.

No way. I woke up there one night in absolute terror, trapped in my mind and screaming for a way out. Only where the hell was I supposed to go? I had no idea whose room I was in! Whose house was this?

Had I unconsciously broken into someone's home in the middle of the night? What if they came home and found me? Would they shoot me or something? Was there anyone else in the house that would be able to draw a bead on me and kill me right then if I screamed? I had to get out immediately.

Only how do you get out of a house in the dark when you don't know your way around?

I looked toward the window and frantically pulled the curtains back, slapping the glass while looking for a door or opening somewhere. Nothing. I turned and in the midst of a panic attack tried to stay as quiet as possible to avoid alerting the anonymous homeowners. At the same time, I was also hurriedly making my way through the house. I smashed into the dining room table with such force that I thought I'd castrated myself. If someone else was in here, they were going to find me for sure. I had to get out! I couldn't let them kill me, so I kept looking for light coming in from windows until I finally located a door to escape.

I got outside and saw my car. I'd driven here. This was Jay's house. Jay and Christy were gone. Getting married. It all started coming back. I was here to watch their house and take care of their cat.

The cat!

This was a house cat, and I'd been given explicit instructions to not let the cat out.

Now here I was, in the middle of a black night, in my boxers and bare feet in the middle of a driveway. Only when I'd run out, I'd been in such a panic that I hadn't stopped to close the door behind me.

Oh, no!

Ask yourself, what you would do if you were a cat and some raving lunatic suddenly started pounding your windows and smashing tables against his nuts in the middle of the night? Would you be a little unsettled?

Yeah, well so was Telachi the cat.

I had the "fantastic" luck that Telachi just happened to be completely black, so finding him in the midst of a moonless night wasn't quite as bad as finding a needle in a haystack, but it was pretty close.

After I'd spent probably the better part of forty-five minutes looking for him throughout the house and around the yard, I surrendered myself to the possibility that he'd already been devoured by one the canyon coyotes, and I'd have to share my incompetent pet protection methods with Jay and Christy once they returned. This could blow my whole façade of normalcy.

Then I remembered Christy had left treats for me to give to Telachi. Once I retrieved those, simply shaking the treat bowl did the trick, and the little guy meowed. He was huddled right over near the front door, a little frightened looking, and had probably been hanging out close to the house the entire time. Ironically, he seemed just as scared of the big, unfamiliar night as I'd been just a little while before.

The next day I finally decided to call one of the rehab centers Dr. Ludwig had recommended.

These incidents happened quite often, and I was aware they needed to be stopped. Although they happened a lot in my sleep, they also hap-pened while I was tired. I knew they were getting the better of me, and since they were also getting worse, maybe this was something a rehab facil-ity could help me with.

I called the number and a woman answered. I told her who I was, and she introduced herself as Lisa. She couldn't have been any more pleas-ant. She was very soft and understanding to my situation and explained the type of services her rehab facility provided. As I listened to her description, I realized that it pretty much all applied to me.

This wasn't good, because it started reinforcing my fears that I was "different" now. The fact that I recognized many of the behaviors she de-scribed, things like a lack of short-term memory, or an inability to focus my vision, an inability to recall info, and so on, meant that again, maybe she was right, Dr. Ludwig was right, Tracy was right, and ultimately Billy had been right. I wasn't myself. I was having problems—way more than what I initially thought I'd have. I just didn't want to face it.

I hung up.

What could I do? She was describing things that brain-injured pa-tients deal with. The fact that I was dealing with all of them, however, was not something I wanted to know. It meant I was, in fact, brain-damaged. Could I finally admit that to myself?

I'd thought it was a possibility for a while, but I'd never really had confirmation. Even when Dr. Ludwig diagnosed me, he never came right out and said, "Yo, loser, you're brain-damaged." His language was very nonconfrontational. "You have a post-concussive disorder." It had helped me at the time that he'd been that way, and I'm sure he'd learned through the years to talk to people like myself in ways that wouldn't upset them or send them running for the door.

But Lisa, for all her kindness, had upset me. She'd confirmed my biggest fears, and for all the help she said she could give, it was the last thing I wanted. I knew she didn't mean to hurt me, but how else could I respond?

I wanted to be like my old self again. Who was I now? I didn't know. I wanted to be like everyone else. I didn't want to have to take drugs to make me stable. I didn't want to wake up screaming in the middle of the night. I didn't want any of the weird stuff I was experiencing. And yet, here I was. I couldn't deny it—I was dealing with it.

*I*N THE MID 1970s, *my dad was temporarily laid off by GM.*

My Uncle Bill was also laid off by his construction company, so when a job became available for him in Florida, Aunt Carol and Uncle Bill took my cousins and moved there. Then there was another position available, and Uncle Bill called my dad about it. Fairly quickly, Dad was in Ft. Lauderdale doing construction work, and a few weeks later, he flew my mom and me down to be with him.

The whole experience lasted less than a year, but it made a huge impression on me. As much as anything, it showed me there was a whole different world outside of Flint—a world that had little to do with cars. In Florida, oranges and coconuts and speedboats and the ocean were as big as anything I'd experienced.

My cousin Billy was three months older than me and therefore the first best friend and playmate I'd ever had. We made friends with a boy named Bubba, who was a few years older than us. Bubba treated us like his own little brothers and protected us when we needed it. He cemented the friendship deal by giving us a Batman and Robin record, which captivated Billy and me no end, except that we didn't know how to play the record. Anyhow, he'd given us a Batman record, and I had a huge crush on Bubba's sister Tanya, so I made sure I was around Bubba's house as often as possible.

Florida was fun, but it wasn't to last. General Motors called my dad back to work, and we made plans to head back to Flint. Only this time, we weren't going to drive straight up I-75. No, Uncle Dave had taken a job in Texas, so we decided to drive from Florida to see him. This would be my first experience traveling the country by car, and I found it electrifying after so much time with my puzzle map back home. Along the way, there were so many sites to see. We stopped at Busch Gardens and the Everglades, and made our way across Alabama, Mississippi, and Louisiana right into the home state of the cowboys I'd learned about, also known as the "Lone Star State."

Uncle Dave seemed to be doing well, and it was neat to see him as a grown-up making a life of his own somewhere outside Flint. Uncle Dave was in Texas, so to me he was like a cowboy now!

From there, I remember the trip back north and falling asleep to the car radio each night as my parents and I wound our way toward Michigan.

This trip was significant in that it was probably the first time I felt total peace and contentment with my mom and dad the way I had with Grandpa and Grandma Goss. I don't know what it was about the road that lulled me to that place of security, but I loved the feel of it all and the connection to my family and the country and something so much bigger than myself. To this day, I have a serenity that overtakes me when I hear Roberta Flack's "Killing Me Softly" from all the times I heard it back then—it's almost Pavlovian.

I remember the roadside motels with the "100% Refrigerated Air," and even the "fancy" Holiday Inns we'd sometimes stay at. How great they were! Who wouldn't want to feel refrigerated air, especially in the humid summer of the American South? The inground swimming pools my dad would take me in at night had exciting lights that twinkled beneath the water unlike any aboveground pool I'd seen back home but very much like the beautiful lights behind the Stepping Stone Falls back in Flint. There were diners and restaurants along the roads that had personalities unlike anything back in Flint, and yet, somehow the people were the same in the kindnesses they'd offer to anyone who simply needed breakfast or a cup of coffee. While I'm not completely certain of it, it's altogether possible—and even likely—that after leaving Texas on our way back to Michigan, this early '70s trip marked the first time that I ever heard the hum of Route 66 below me. I'm not sure of when or in what states that would have occurred, but whatever it was about the sights, sounds, and feel of the road, I was hypnotized.

I remember being thrilled by the fact that for some distance along our trip, the rail line ran right alongside the road we were on. I was enthralled the first time a train came up alongside us. I'm sure marine biologists must feel the same way when they swim beside a whale for the first time, but for me, to be in tandem with the trains was one of the most spectacular experiences of my life. They were so mammoth beside our Buick, and the lumbering sound of their engines powering over railroad ties, stones, and steel made a sound that invigorated me like no other. The night my dad decided to race one of the trains was probably the first time I'd ever tasted adrenaline. How could it be possible to beat a fast and powerful train? And yet my dad did, which only contributed to the beginning of a legend that he was a superhero who could be beaten by nothing—not man, beast, or machine. My dad beating that train may have also been my first experience with believing that within my family, I could do anything too.

Ten

~

"Next Door to the Blues"

I WAS brain-damaged.

So what about my six months of recovery from a post-concussive disorder? I decided that I needed to see Dr. Ludwig again before I committed to any rehab facilities. He could give me the information I was looking for. Yes, that was it.

Dr. Ludwig and I went through another battery of tests before he talked with me. He checked my progress and wanted to know how I thought things were going. I neglected to tell him about the panic attacks, but I shared my concerns that the six months was up. He shared an addendum I didn't want to hear.

Post-concussive disorder generally rights itself within six months, but it can easily last a year, and in some cases longer. If it were longer, Dr. Ludwig told me that he'd reassess what I needed at that time. Maybe some things wouldn't go away entirely. Maybe I'd have some permanent change from my accident. The only thing that could tell was time.

He asked how the drugs were working, and since I didn't want to be questioned about why I wasn't taking them, I told him I thought they were "okay."

But he didn't give up.

He asked me which antidepressant I'd started on, since he'd given me an array of choices to try.

I told him I didn't remember, and I'm sure he knew at this point that I was lying about the whole thing.

Anyhow, I'm sure he'd been through this whole patient paranoia before, and because he's absolutely brilliant, he didn't push me in a way that would make me never come back or eventually avoid getting the help I'd need. Dr. Ludwig also knew I'd lost my job. He knew my financial situation. He offered me more samples of antidepressants with the encouragement that they'd stabilize me more, and he told me to let him know if I had any weird reactions to them.

I honestly didn't know. My condition had been amended to last a lot longer than I was prepared for, and until it was done, I didn't think I could find a job I'd be able to maintain. At the same time, Lisa had offered me a way out. Unfortunately, I didn't want to accept that I was brain-damaged, whether I was or not. I convinced myself that I was still able to do most of what I'd always done, so why would I suddenly go to a rehab facility? I was still driving—though in hindsight, not well. I was still able to carry a conversation—I just couldn't sustain it, and I was still able to think rationally—yeah, right. But this is what I told myself.

I decided to keep pushing along on my lonesome, but maybe, as long as no one else knew, maybe I should consider taking one of the anti-depressants. This was discouraging because not only didn't I want to admit I was brain-damaged, I also didn't want to admit I was depressed. Again, I was caught up in the condemnation of all the "depression" patients I'd worked with on the psych ward. They were the most frustrating patients because they were their own worst enemies. You'd motivate them toward something, and they'd refuse to take the motivation. It seemed that they chose their own poison. I surely wasn't like that! Was I?

It didn't matter. I was where I was. I told myself that I wasn't as bad as any of them had been. I was only depressed because I was unable to control my panic, process information, sleep and understand other people—little things, you know? Still, if I could get the boost I needed from taking these drugs, maybe all would be forgiven. Once I got better, I could tell myself I'd only used a temporary solution to get back to my permanent, normal state. Yes, that was it.

I went home that day and stood with one of the sample boxes in my hand. I didn't know which of the three was best for me to take, but Dr. Ludwig had been clear that I should stick with just one brand at a time so I could see how that particular brand affected me over a three-week period.

I ripped open the box and slid out the silver tab of pills. I pressed one of the tablets against its tin foil retainer compartment until it snapped free into my hand.

I stood there looking at it.

Once I took this, I knew it would affect my drug-free history on earth. Why that mattered so much, I don't know, but it meant that I'd need-ed drugs to make myself normal. By taking it, I was admitting to myself that I wasn't normal anymore. If I didn't take it, I wouldn't have to admit that fact.

Eleven

~

"If You Walkin' Alone"

T HE REPRIEVE AFTER TAKING the drugs wasn't a reprieve at all. I was still waking up with panic attacks at night. During the day, while my mood did become less up and down, it stabilized at such a low level that I was still tired all the time. I didn't have much motivation, either.

Before the end of the second week on the drugs, I'd begun spending all day in bed watching TV. Some days I didn't get up at all. This was worse than before.

The thing that broke me out of it was that I'd registered with a church to go on a whitewater rafting trip in central California. I'd paid for it long before, and being truthful, even in the mental state I was in, it seemed like it would be fun. I'd done this when I was a kid with my dad and some of his friends, and it had always been a good time. This was the first chance I'd had to do it in California, though, so I was excited to see the difference in West Coast versus East Coast thrills. Maybe it was the boost I needed to get going again. I told myself that, anyway.

I don't remember how it worked, but true to my absentminded form, when I registered, I'd forgotten to sign up for a tent to sleep in. I'd signed up for a carpool on the way up, but once I got there, I was out of luck for sleeping arrangements. There were about sixty people registered, so I hoped I could find at least one person who had room in a tent for me.

I was fortunate, then, to get assigned to a carpool with a guy who happened to have a four-man tent and only himself signed up to sleep in it. He offered almost straightaway that if I needed a place to crash, there'd be plenty of room in his tent. I was happy about that since it took one element of stress out of the picture instantly.

Any element of stress in the life of a brain-injured patient is way more crippling than in the life of a normal-minded person. Stress and its sometimes inevitable results—frustration and anger—can suck the life right out of you in a way that will leave you flat for an entire day. You have to be really careful not to fall into situations that bring on these emotions.

I'd been offered a place to sleep, so I could now relax and enjoy the trip. Added to this was the fact that I already knew the guy I was carpooling with. We weren't great friends or anything, but I think it's fair to say we were friendly acquaintances. He was a good old boy, not unlike Cooter from the old Dukes of Hazzard TV show.

When we got up to the river, there were a whole host of campsite choices where he could choose to put up his tent, but for some reason, he chose one on a slight hill in the midst of a bunch of other tents. I guess he was looking forward to the feeling of community from being near so many other friends. All I could think was that being so close to them meant we'd be kept awake by everyone's snoring. That is, if I could even get to sleep in the first place.

I was surprised that night because I fell asleep easily. I'd strategically planned to go to bed earlier than most people, so if I were able, I'd fall asleep first. I am and always have been an extremely heavy sleeper, so I knew if I got to sleep before anyone else, you could have brought in a herd of elephants and I wouldn't have woken up. I'd once slept through an entire fire alarm and drill in my college dorm.

A while later, the worst possible thing happened. I woke up having a panic attack. Only this was no normal panic attack. I woke with my face smashed into some material as if a bag had been placed over my face, and my whole body shoved into a cocoon. Literally, I was pinned from the front and behind. The inevitable question ran through my head ... where the hell was I? What was happening?

I didn't know, but I knew I could breathe.

I realized that wherever I was, I was outside. I seemed to be in a tent, and my face was shoved from the inside out against one of the tent walls. Clearly, I'd slid or rolled down our tent hill into the side of the tent, but the most horrifying part came next.

I heard snoring behind me ... right behind me.

Old Cooter had turned in for the night, and he'd also slid down the tent hill, against me, and he was now sleepily spooning me into the side of the tent.

I didn't even realize who it was, I levitated right out of there, and just as I'd done against the glass at Jay's house, I slapped the tent sides, looking for a way out until I found one. I'm surprised I didn't take the whole thing down in my frantic rush to escape, but I didn't. I eventually sprung from the tent, gasping in the fresh night air.

It was then I realized that the panicked noise I'd been making had drawn the attention of the twenty or so people still sitting around the campfire for the evening. All of them were now staring at me, nearly naked in my boxer shorts and gasping heavily. I realized pretty quickly where I was. Church group. Camping trip.

I went back inside the tent and found my jeans. Cooter was still snoring soundly. At least one of us was resting comfortably.

I sat embarrassed for a moment, trying to figure out whether I should stay there until I fell asleep again or if I should join the crowd I'd just mortified with my near-naked butt.

I went for a third option. I'd take a walk in the night air until my breathing calmed and my pulse settled.

I congratulated myself on handling the situation as well as I did. I hadn't screamed at the top of my lungs, and I'd extricated myself from the tent without waking "Sleeping Beauty."

I seemed to be getting the hang of these panic attacks. Regardless, I eventually went back and resumed my night's sleep in the tent. By that time, Cooter had slid the rest of the way into the tent side, his own face sucking nylon now. Interestingly enough, it did nothing to squelch his snoring.

Fortunately for me, the rest of the night was uneventful, and the next morning, Cooter didn't know what had happened, which was fine by me.

I know for a fact that I didn't know the difference between "white" and "black" until at least around the age of four or five because I remember watching the TV show Sanford and Son with my mom and thinking Fred G. Sanford was white like me, while his son Lamont was black like the folks around my Grandma and Grandpa Goss's house. It didn't strike me as odd that a white man had a black son; it just seemed that some of us were darker or lighter than others. Certainly, the people in my family had lighter and darker complexions than each other, so why couldn't it be possible for Fred to be white and Lamont to be black and still be father and son?

It didn't take long to notice that racial and cultural differences seemed to be the only things anyone wanted to talk about. People who'd previously remained silent finally let their words bubble over. Phrases like "There goes the neighborhood" entered the popular culture, and like many kids, I'm sure I picked up on being "different" from black children. That, of course, robs the innocence of a kid a little bit. It also instills a fear of what you don't know, but I was different from the white kids I was around in that I wasn't afraid. Unlike the white kids in my new hometown, I'd been around black kids at Grandpa and Grandma Goss's house, and I didn't see the big deal or difference. I wanted to learn what I could about the world, and certainly in my family, I'd been encouraged to explore and learn as much as I could. There was no question I couldn't ask, and generally no answer I wasn't given. So I grew up in sort of a dual existence of being the only white kid in my grandparents' neighborhood, while also know-ing exactly what the one black family felt like in the town I lived in with my parents. Meanwhile, the climate of tension and fear between the races seemed ever-present all around me.

During the brief time that we lived in Florida, I had my first taste of what racism was, and it was an ugly one. Aunt Carol and Uncle Bill's kids were all close in age to me, and my favorite cousin Billy had made a best friend in a boy named Ira at his school. One afternoon, he invited Ira over to swim in our apartment complex's pool with us, and Ira also invited his brothers and sisters to come with him. This should have been fine since they were all small children around the age of five years old.

There was one problem, however. Ira and his siblings were black, and when they arrived, all the adults in our apartment complex let them know it. Never in my life, before or since, have I seen a more horrific display of hatred than when a bunch of adults shouted cruelly from balconies and parking lots for the "niggers" to go home.

I remember watching Ira's face fall. In an instant, he went from being an equal playmate with Billy and me to being something these hateful grown-ups saw as less than human. Without words, he and his brothers and sisters ran away to safety through the coconut grove and back across the sand field that separated the middle-class white section from the poor black section in Ft. Lauderdale. That was traumatic for me, and I know it was even more traumatic for him. Ira and his family never came back to play with us again, although we were always accepted when we went to his side of the sand field.

Around the same time, I learned that there were more than just the color differences between blacks and whites in Ft. Lauderdale. There was also a group known as "Mexicans," and they weren't as dark as blacks or as light as whites, but rather looked like a mix of both groups. Somehow though, this group wasn't only allowed to swim in our apartment complex pool, they actually lived among us in the apartments. There was one big Mexican family living across from us, and we'd often play with their kids. One of the older boys was constantly threatening to beat me up, though, so I tried to make sure I was only around him when my cousins or Bubba were there to protect me. I didn't understand why he'd want to beat me up simply because I was lighter than he was, but this racism seemed like a bunch of malarkey.

The whole era seemed like a catharsis of different tensions that had built up and had not been expressed for the previous two hundred years.

The other phenomenon of the time was that suddenly people were getting divorced left and right simply because they could, when twenty years previous, no one would have even conceived of it. Women were increasingly banging the gong of equality and making the news with their demonstrations for independence and equal rights. The country was furious with the corruption in government, and the long-haired hippie Vietnam vets that hitchhiked from place to place were treated as pariahs by everyone. The government didn't like the hippies, and the short-haired people who didn't like the corrupt government didn't like the drug addict behavior of these burned-out vagabonds, either. It seemed that just about everyone was mad at someone else about something. I just couldn't understand where it had all come from and I missed the safety and stability I'd known back in Michigan. Everyone in my family loved and looked out for each other, though, so in that regard, things were still all right for me.

I imagine for anyone else, in a less loving, less stable family, things had probably gone quite crazy. Jumping on one of those trains bound for who-knew-where out of whatever town they were in at the moment may have seemed like the most attractive option of all. It just seemed that every-one was trying to escape whatever life they lived.

Twelve

~

"Dweller on the Threshold"

I BECAME VERY temperamental. Very moody. Very irritable and frustrated. Think of the most sleep-deprived, grouchiest condition you've ever been in and multiply it by ten.

I started to get double vision. Not always, mind you, but if I got tired or stressed on top of my massive headaches, I had crazy dizziness from it and a poor sense of balance. When I wasn't simply dizzy, without energy, and depressed in my bed, I was frustrated and angry toward the world over the smallest things. More than that, I'd lie there ruminating, almost searching for things to get angry about. It was becoming more and more of a problem as time went by.

I'd fix the blame on my old boss for putting me in this position. How could someone who had once called me a friend cast me out when I needed friendship and support the most? In fairness, in the years since then, my other boss, Billy, told me he didn't think his partner even knew I was hurt. He just wasn't focused on me or understanding about my situation.

Anger is extremely common to sufferers of brain injuries with major depression. Had I not been depressed over the seeming indifference of my former boss, I would have attached my depression to some other cause.

And that's the thing. Since depression routinely accompanies a brain injury, it was easy to hook the cause of it to my old boss, but the truth is that it was the injury itself. I'm sure losing my job didn't help matters, but I want to be very clear that if you've been injured, depression is a normal side effect. You could call depression one of the brain's natural responses to someone smacking it. Not unlike that girl on the playground who'd cry predictably when her pigtails got pulled—a natural response to inflicted pain.

I can't really get too upset at my boss, though, because the way he treated me is indicative of the larger societal problem of not understanding brain injuries. I was messing up, and he cut me from the team—simple. But since he had once called me his friend, it hurt because I'd thought I'd been pretty close with not just him but his entire family. I had needed that feeling of "family support" right about then. After all, I didn't have many other loved ones to choose from at the time.

I was alone and needed someone I could really rely on and trust to be there for me. In the past, my boss and his family would have stepped forward to fill the void. We'd been real friends. I'd have been content if they'd just shown some basic concern. I needed support and affirmation that I was going to be all right. The fact that I didn't have anyone like that left me feeling really alone.

And before you ask, yes, I did have other friends. I was just so paranoid and self-conscious that I didn't feel like I could spend any substantial time with them because they'd figure out what was going on with me. If that happened, I ran the risk of my old friends looking at me—or worse, thinking of me—differently.

Didn't it make sense that if they thought differently of me, we wouldn't have the same kind of friendship anymore? Wouldn't it become a relationship based on pity or charity? I certainly didn't want that, but who else could I turn to, if not my friends? What would the prognosis be if they found out about me and the friendship dissolved, and then I recovered later? I didn't want to lose friendships that I might be able to resume once I was better. So I hid myself away from them all. Telling my real family didn't seem like the right thing to do, either.

When you live 2,500 miles from your family, and you're in the midst of a crisis you can't understand, inciting their worry is pointless. Instead, I chose to act toward them the way I did with everyone else—I faked it. On occasions we might be on the phone, and any of them asked how I was doing after my accident, I generally just kept it topical or said I was "Okay."

How do you say anything else? At first, I didn't know there was anything wrong with me, so to go back and say, "Remember when I said I was 'okay' all those times? Well …" It seemed like a lot of useless talk if I couldn't tell them what was actually wrong. The truth was, I didn't understand it myself. More than that, I wasn't aware of all that was happening. My perceptions were very subjective and made a lot more sense to me than they did to the people around me. In the past, I've used the quote "The world made sense to me, but I didn't make sense to the world." That pretty much describes it.

From what people still tell me today about my behavior back then, I seemed to be perfectly content acting in very bizarre ways. I didn't even always know I was being weird, and when you don't know you're a little "off," how do you let others know, let alone your family? Ultimately, the biggest conundrum I faced was how to tell people I wasn't okay when I couldn't figure it out for myself—or worse, wasn't even willing to admit it to myself. I was stuck in a bind.

I continued to bumble along, but the thing that upset me most was feeling like I didn't have anyone to lean on: someone who could physically be there to help me talk through my confusion. That's why it's so important to be supportive of people who have suffered brain injuries. Most of the time, we have very few people to talk to. If we choose you, it's because you are really someone extremely special to us.

I suppose that's why I put so much importance on my boss and his family. I knew they could be there for me and had been previously, in fact. It was just a matter of whether they wanted to be now. As they were the only friends I had who'd witnessed what had happened to me from the beginning and the subsequent changes after the accident, I hoped they'd keep our friendship on the table, even if our working relationship was over. But without understanding or knowing what I was going through, not only was the working relationship over, the friendship was murdered too, and that sent me further into depression.

Friendship has always been an important part of my life, and my longtime good friends know I'm loyal like no other. I'm the guy who, even if you haven't talked to me in ten years, you could call in the middle of the night to bail you out of a Mexican jail and feel safe knowing no one would ever find out. I might razz you over the next few years for comedy purposes, but what's a little humor over jail time between friends, right?

In any case, my boss's indifference really impacted me a lot more than it should have. As I'd been friends with him and his whole family, to not hear from any of them just gave me a whole cavalcade of people to negatively focus my troubles on.

Anything was better than focusing on myself.

I think that's because I didn't know where to focus. My situation didn't make sense, so how did I get a grasp of it? It was easier to just pin it all on someone else. That's what an unhealthy person does.

Regardless of the dynamics of my feelings over the whole situation, the distorted thinking from my injury certainly wasn't helping me see things any more clearly. All I knew was that I was hurting. Why had they abandoned me? I was obsessive about it.

That's another aspect to brain injuries. You obsess over the stupidest things and blow up over the smallest things. Worse yet, you tend to treat the smallest things as if they're the biggest. It's very common to act in a stupid manner and feel completely justified in doing so.

I will admit, though, that even to this day, one thing about being treated so indifferently back then still hurts.

As George Bernard Shaw said: "The opposite of love isn't hate, it's indifference," and I have to say … I totally agree.

Thirteen

~

"Lonely Avenue"

WHAT I NEEDED MOST was social contact, not isolation, but the amount of damage that getting worked up emotionally wrought on my body was anything but pleasant. So, given the choice between spending emotional time with friends or spending time alone in the peaceful quiet—it wasn't much of a choice. I needed as much peace as I could get from what was becoming an increasingly torturous existence.

Emotions are a funny thing to a brain-injured person. I don't think I'd be out of line to say that I began to feel everything on a super-powered level. I didn't know why I was becoming this way, but I did know that my emotions fluctuated wildly, and any emotion at all was likely to be experienced at a high level, and the energy I expended feeling it would leave me totally exhausted.

To some people, a man who can be regularly emotional probably sounds like a dream. Trust me, though, the extent to which I experienced my emotions was devastating; it was another new gift from the accident that just kept on giving. Now I was unable to control or monitor my feelings.

One minute I'd be down-in-the-dumps depressed, and the next minute I'd be jubilantly happy, often at inappropriate levels. If I was out somewhere and had the good luck to be laughing with people, I'd sometimes hear people say, "It's not that funny, Dan," and I'd instantly know my injury was showing. But how do you come back from that? Argue with them about whether or not something is funny?

That would have been one way to handle things, and it was probably not outside the realm of possibilities, as my temper would skyrocket in seconds and make me want to fight it out. Before my accident, if I thought someone was being mean or inappropriate, I might have let it slide, whereas after my accident, that seemed nearly impossible. I wanted to fight—a lot.

And the fact that I'd kept working out in the gym didn't help the other guy's chances much, either. With my anger thrown on top of it, let's just say, I feel bad for some of the things I did.

I don't know that it'd be wrong to say I was like a baby in the way my emotions governed me. If I felt happy, I laughed uncontrollably. If I felt sad, I cried until there were no more tears. If I felt angry, I'd throw a tantrum so big that you could hear me for ten city blocks.

Around this time, oddly enough, I remember that customer service people used to really tick me off like no one else could. I mean, I'd really lose it with them.

And before I get into this further, let me first just say this: Customer service sucks anyway.

I remember a time when an error was made on one of my bills— a bill I'd already paid. I called the customer service rep, and on the other end of the line, I found all the intellect of a can of soup. These people are tough to deal with for a normal-minded person. Can you imagine throwing a brain injury into the mix? Hopeless! Anyhow, on this particular day, I'd called about a paid bill that had been marked unpaid, and the person didn't want to understand, and they didn't try, all things that a normal-minded person would expect and would work through. The problem was that I wasn't normal-minded at the time, and my coping skills were just below nonexistent.

I blew up.

My roommate had gotten quite used to my blow-ups, but I could tell my temper made him nervous. It was almost as if the silent question had been asked, "When are these explosions going to turn physical against me?" There was a real vibe of "I might need physical protection from this psychopath soon" that floated on the air in our place, and I tried my best not to acknowledge it.

The truth is, I didn't know if that question had any validity because my temper was getting worse, and I didn't know how to explain away my behavior to him. After all, the things I'd get upset about were sensible things to be bothered about. At the same time, the extent to which I'd get angry would be so over the top in regards to what was expected or appropriate that I couldn't justify it. Worse yet, I couldn't stop it. Once my temper approached the runway, it wouldn't even roll to a stop. It would just keep on going and, with all the power of a jet engine, it would zoom skyward and not stop until I was in outer space, often until I was just beyond Uranus.

It really was like an out-of-body experience. I could see how animated or rageful I appeared. I didn't know why I was so full of fury, but I had no ability to regulate it.

I'd tried boxing a bit before my accident, but truthfully, I'd never really been a violent person. That was changing now, however. The fact that

I could objectively look at myself from the outside and see that I was acting in scary ways did nothing to stop me from being that way. I simply couldn't do anything about it. Once my temper was gone, I felt powerless to do anything but let it run its course.

Clearly, this was a problem when blending in with normal society. For some silly reason, people aren't all that thrilled at having loose cannons firing off random volleys just because they happen on to some unexpected powder. I didn't know what to do, but I did know I was behaving inappropriately. I decided that from then on, if I started getting angry, I needed to get away from people. I'd go to my bed, to my car, or to wherever I needed to go that was completely private and away from others.

And yes, you read that right. I said "my car," and yes, I was still driving. For all the stuff going on in my head—my lack of judgment, my emotional nature, my horrible temper—none of these things kept me from keeping a valid California driver's license.

I'd finally graduated to "insane L.A. driver."

I'm exaggerating a bit because I had firm rules for myself. I never went over the speed limit and I'd always keep at least three to four car lengths between me and the next car. I'd often leave early if I needed to get somewhere, and in this way, I was never in a rush, something that often leads to frustrated drivers and victims of road rage. In this way, I had it under control. In fact, I was probably my most normal when driving in traffic.

That said, I might still completely zone out and run through several red lights, stop at greens or nearly run down pedestrians. Yes, yes ... I did plenty of that. Fortunately, I never caused any tragedies.

However, the most important thing is that, just like when I was a child lulled to sleep by the hum of the road, when I was behind the wheel, I felt a sense of peace. Calm. No rage. No nothing. Just peace. The fact that there was even such a place like that was beyond comforting for me.

Fortunately for the local pedestrians, I couldn't really afford gas without a job, so driving all the time wasn't an option. I was forced to spend time with myself at home, and that was becoming increasingly difficult. Not only did life stop making sense, I'd stopped liking myself. I was exhausted all the time from my sporadic sleep schedule, and I was afraid to be around people in case I created a situation that became irreversibly embarrassing.

I mean, if there was any fear about people finding out I was different now and treating me like I was retarded, it was nothing compared to the fear I had about freaking out and going ballistic in front of all of them. I'd never been particularly good when I was upset, but now I was also dangerous. My thinking was that if I really wanted to have no friends, it would just be a matter of time before I'd have an explosion around one or more of them that would virtually guarantee it.

I really can't caution you enough on this: It's not wise to upset a person who's been brain-injured. With no ego-based governor in place to stop them, they're apt to be about as unpredictable as a rattlesnake in a rat's nest. You will get bitten—possibly even eaten.

If you think you hear even the slightest sound of a rattlesnake's rattle, make tracks. Either that, or start being so nice they can't possibly be upset with you. Wear a Ronald McDonald mask, maybe. After all, who could be mad at Ronald McDonald?

Then again, with logic like that (which is mostly nonexistent anyway), you don't even have to do anything wrong to incur a brain-injured person's wrath. They may just imagine you being involved in something bad toward them, and that's all you'll need to be in the way, way, way wrong place at the way, way, way wrong time.

ONCE MY FAMILY AND I HAD *returned to Michigan and my dad was back to work in the good old auto plant, I was just glad we'd gotten back to what we'd had before. What we had in Flint was better than in the other places in the country, and it was definitely a solid, dependable life. I didn't know what life would be like for those people back in Florida or elsewhere in the country, but in Michigan, thank God, it was still good for us.*

It didn't take long before the conflicts of the 1970s started to permeate everything. With everything going on in society, I guess it was only a matter of time before it hit our family too. The normalcy of life in Flint got knocked off its foundation with the energy crisis, as well as the "gas-guzzler" label that had been aimed at our cars by the new Japanese car manufacturers—and, of course, the arrival of those Japanese cars themselves. At first, everyone was a little too smart to fall for this obvious attempt to steal some of the market with cheap, tiny tin-can cars, which is exactly what they were when they arrived on the scene.

The fact that anyone would even think of buying a Japanese car at that time, let alone actually doing it, was almost considered treasonous. Our country was entering a recession, and the fact that every dollar mattered and was tight for folks meant that buying a foreign car and sending those vanishing dollars permanently overseas to strengthen the economies of foreign countries was only going to make us weaker. It was anti-American.

Still, it had started happening in other parts of the country, and all that any of us in Michigan could do was hope Americans who were buying foreign-made cars would come to their senses and invest their dollars back in our economy. If they did, our country would regain its strength, and our own companies across the country would be able to kick production back into gear because they'd have the money to do so. Jobs would be created again because there would be a renewed interest in American products that would demand more workers to make them.

And yet for some reason, according to the nightly news reports on the economy, this didn't seem to be happening. Before long, I saw the first Japanese cars trickling onto our streets, and it definitely got other people's attention, too. It was yet another element to create tension in a time when tension already seemed to be going through the roof.

With all the sneering and anger toward everyone going around me, my idyllic life in Michigan was far from what it had been, and it was even further from the glamour and bright lights of Chicago.

Just when I wanted to rest in the knowledge that I was at least on solid ground with my family in Flint, my grandparents shook me with an earthquake. I guess the '70s finally got to them too.

Around 1975, Grandpa and Grandma Goss decided they were going to get divorced. It was unheard of for people of their generation, but they were going to do it. Although I'd heard the term, I didn't really know what it meant, but I quickly found out. The safe, stable home I'd known with them was no more. The divorce was an extremely bitter one that I didn't understand because I'd never seen them be cruel to each other before. Not that it didn't happen, I guess, but it had never happened in front of me. Anyhow, when all was said and done, Grandpa Goss was gone. Not much was said about it to us grandkids, but the odd thing was that no one really said anything more about him at all—he was just gone.

The worst part was that when each of their kids supported my grandma instead of my grandpa, they completely estranged themselves from him. And when they broke off contact with him, it meant I lost him too. That hurt—deeply. I think it ripped an element of trust from my heart that told me I couldn't keep faith in the people around me to do what might be right for me when they had the opportunity to do what was best for them instead. I learned my own needs might be forgotten, which woke me up pretty quickly to who and what was important to me, as well as to the importance of taking care of myself and fighting for what I wanted.

However, I did what any kid would do with such a loss of stability: I invested in the only other safe place I had, which was at home with my parents.

I developed quite a fear that something would happen and they'd end up gone too. My dad would leave for work in his blue Chevy pickup, and as he drove the two miles down our rural country road toward the state highway, I'd run out into the road and watch as his truck became smaller and smaller in the distance. That was my dad, I thought, and keeping him in eyesight for as long as I possibly could before he disappeared became a regular practice for me. I just hoped to see him again. He was strong, and he was my dad, and no matter what, I didn't want to lose him.

But once the dominos started to fall, they just didn't stop, and in 1977, my mom and dad decided to get divorced too. Just after that, my Aunt Carol and Uncle Bill, who had long ago returned from Florida with my cousins, decided they hated each other like everyone else, so they got divorced as well. It was like an epidemic. My family was imploding, and it was terrifying. Everything was changing so fast, and I didn't seem able to do anything about it. I wanted one place that was stable and familiar. Only, the more I wanted it, the more elusive a place like that seemed to become.

In those last few years of the '70s, something else was happening. General Motors began laying people off. And then they laid off more. And more. They laid people off until about eighty thousand jobs had been displaced.

Prior to the massive number of layoffs, I'd compare Flint to a town like Burbank, California. Not because it was sunny and tropical but because it had been fast-paced, progressive, and had a cool vibe that made it a fun place to be. The auto industry was our movie industry; it was our pride and joy. If the auto industry was gone, what would be left of any of our lives? Not much, it seemed.

Fourteen

~

"Road Block"

EVERY DAY IT SEEMED LIKE I was dealing with something new. Not only were my panic attacks as predictable as any alarm clock, my temper was even more alarming than the clock. Beyond the other normal struggles of social isolation, lack of consistent sleep, depression, inability to read or process information, little communication comprehension, and deficiencies in regulating my emotions, I was also losing other knowledge.

Forget the simple days of not knowing how to make copies of computer disks; I was on to bigger things, like finding whole sections of my memory gone.

I'd played basketball for two years way back in junior high school. I was never great, which is why I didn't play in high school, but I knew how to play the game. I loved to watch it even more, and growing up in Michigan during the days of the back-to-back NBA Championship–winning Detroit Pistons of '89 and '90, you know I was a fan. Those were also the days of a young Michael Jordan, and finding a player like that to watch, how could you not be captivated by this game?

I remember during the spring after my accident, while watching a game in Los Angeles, I suddenly realized I no longer had a clue about what was happening on the court.

How did this game work?

I knew they were trying to put the orange ball in the hoop at either end, but what about all those guys on the court? How exactly were they organized to make that happen?

This was bad. I'd been one of those guys—a point guard, actually—and I'd known the rules. Now I sat there trying to make sense of where those rules had gone. Moreover, I had visual memory of being on the court, but I had no recall of what the rules were when I'd been there. Remember the dream analogy I used about flying the plane? I had memory of it, but not the technical ability to do or understand it. It was the same with basketball. And of course, without technical ability, skill was gone too, because, as we know, the higher someone's technical ability, the more skillful they can be. The converse of this holds true; that is, with no technical ability, there is no skill. I'd lost the ability and skill to understand or play basketball, just the same as if someone had literally stolen it from me. It was just gone.

It carried over to baseball too. A female friend with a command of sports knowledge that rivals any man I know put me and another friend to the test. Did we know the seven ways to get on base in baseball? I remember just standing there. I had no clue what she was talking about. Which sport was baseball? As usual, I faked it.

When our mutual friend made a guess, I'd repeat his answer directly afterward to make it seem like I was coming up with the same answers, just a half-second slower.

Again, this total blank was from a Michigan guy who grew up watching the dominant Detroit Tiger teams of the '80s, most specifically, the 1984 World Champions. Even my mom, who wasn't a huge sports fan, knew about the Tigers. It was the one sport she'd let me watch without any complaint of interrupting her All in the Family reruns. I still remembered my favorite players back then: Dan Petrie, Alan Trammell, Lou Whitaker, Darryl Evans, John Wockenfuss, and my absolute favorites, catcher Lance Parrish and heavy hitter Kirk Gibson. I just knew nothing about the game they played anymore.

I'd also played football in high school. Could I tell you anything about it? Nope. Who was I? Pretty much everything I'd ever defined myself by was changing.

Before my accident, as you know, I'd been a young man from the Midwest who believed in God and did his best to make his family proud. I'd never been a star athlete, but I'd played sports like your average American boy and was involved in the same activities and interests his friends were. I'd been blessed with a vivid imagination, was extremely creative, and had found success as an actor in theater and state organizations by the time I was eighteen. I'd never had trouble with the law or with drugs that indicated future trouble or concern for my parents. Instead, like I said, I'd completed my bachelor's and master's degrees in record time and gone straight into private practice before pursuing a dream in Hollywood. I wanted to know where that guy had gone. My life had turned so cruel.

I couldn't even perform the duties of a basic assistant's job anymore. If you strip a man of even his chance at a career, what's left? Just the man himself? Not even that, because I no longer related to who I'd been. I didn't know who I was—only who I used to be.

Today, I was a depressed, angry, irritable, anxious, fearful, and unemployed recluse. The man I'd been before my accident was totally the opposite of that. How I'd become the antithesis of all I believed in and stood for seemed completely unrealistic and totally implausible.

And yet, it wasn't.

It was what I was facing, and I couldn't ignore it. Everything about whom I'd been and everything bright or good about my life was fading to black.

The way I've described brain injury to people is that it's like being in a room where there's a quick power outage and the lights go out for an instant.

My accident had given me that brief instant of the lights going out, followed quickly by what seemed a restoration of power. A quick check and everything seemed okay. But in the months that followed, it was as if those lights had been instantly reset on a dimmer switch and were now being slowly turned down month by month. What had been clear turned dim, and much of that was now turning dark or was already no longer visible.

My depression was at an all-time high. Instead of my antidepressants making things better, if anything, they'd made things worse. I'd heard about this happening. People who might have been marginal swung the wrong way on drugs, further into darkness, until it devoured them. That didn't seem too far away.

I lay in bed pretty much all day, unable to motivate myself out of it. It didn't make sense to get up if all I had to face was embarrassing myself or getting embarrassed by people learning how pathetic I'd become. I'd rather people remembered me for the way I used to be instead of getting to know me as I was.

Fifteen

~

"Walk a Thin Line"

IN JUNE OF 2003, I decided to kill myself.

The easiest way would be to buy a gun and blast a hole right through where my brain used to be. That would be my ultimate revenge and victory against it.

Since I didn't have a gun, I needed a way I could make this happen. I had access to many guns back in Michigan, but I felt like I couldn't do that to my dad. They were his guns. How could I bring myself to use one of his guns to kill myself? I couldn't. Can you imagine the guilt of knowing you'd purchased the very weapon your only son killed himself with? I couldn't saddle my dad with that.

I'd need to come up with a plan here in L.A. How could I get a handgun? I had a friend that owned quite a few guns, but I knew he'd never part with one, and I was sure that asking to borrow one would sound odd.

This would have to be something I did alone. I'd purchase my own gun. I'd kill myself out of sight of anyone I didn't want to put through the experience of finding me. Of course, this also meant my roommates would have no choice but to find me that way. It didn't seem fair to do that to them, but what choice did I have? I needed a way out.

It's completely common for a brain-injured person to fall into depression and to also have that depression rationally explained away. For example, in the case of a war veteran returning home, a family can easily ascribe the vet's depression to "all he saw in war" rather than to any brain injury he may have suffered while there. Subsequent angry blow-ups or panic attacks can be misdiagnosed as "post-traumatic stress disorder." In the case of married vets, their volatility can be frightening and lead to marital splits that are blamed on how they "changed" because of the war.

All the while, the person is marching steadily toward alcoholism, drug abuse, suicide, and just generally the bottom dropping out of his life due to the aftermath of brain injury.

A lot of research into brain-injured patients and their rehab, recovery, and return to functional life is so new or impossible to access that stats haven't even been compiled, but I'm positive from my experience (and the experiences of the fine folks at the rehab center I eventually went to) that suicidal ideation is not an experience exclusive to me. I know it's all too common to give in to the frustrations, confusion, and shame of not measuring up to what you once were.

That's why I share my desire to kill myself. I want to normalize it somehow because it's just one more shameful thing to have such a selfish desire ascribed to an already injured person. The truth is that this desire really shouldn't be blamed on the person but instead on the brain injury itself because there are tons of brain chemistry regulations and reregulations going on, not to mention all the associated symptoms that arise as a consequence of having an injured or badly functioning brain.

Suicide is only half of it. We can't forget the other half: *homicide*.

In September of 2007, the papers were filled with the headlines about former pro-wrestler Chris Benoit, who in June of 2007 killed his wife, his little boy, and then himself. Postmortem autopsies on his brain revealed damage so significant that doctors described it as looking like the brain of an eighty-year-old. Benoit's brain was filled with abnormal proteins, in fact, the same types of abnormal proteins that were found in the brains of three former NFL players who'd also committed suicide.

It's important to note that doctors admitted that the level of brain damage Benoit had could cause depression and irrational behavior. Is it the type of irrational behavior that causes a man to strangle his wife with a phone cord, his child with a chokehold, and then to hang himself beside a stack of Bibles? Yes, it's exactly that kind because that's just what he did.

I wanted to end the misery. Using a gun seemed the best and quickest way to do it. I'd seen and read too many stories about things going wrong and people ending up still alive but extremely messed up. Can you imagine being more messed up than I already was? That would be too unfair. Using a gun would minimize the room for error by pretty much obliterating any chance of survival.

I had three basic problems at the time: the lack of a weapon, the lack of the stillness of mind necessary to put together a functional plan, and third, the organizational skills of follow-through to actually carry out any plan I might manage to create.

As with the rest of my life at the time, even in this, I was my own worst enemy. For one, I didn't have the energy for the small amount of research necessary to find a good place to buy a gun. There was also the issue of buying one. I hadn't worked in several months, and money wasn't falling off trees. My mom was covering all my bases.

Then there was the issue of whom I'd leave behind.

My mom is such a nice, sweet woman. She's a bit of a talker and a little dramatic at times, but she's also the most good-natured, kind person I know. She loves to laugh. She's also the kind of person who'd literally give her last dime to someone who needed it. She's just that generous. Beyond this, she's lived for nothing but me her entire life. As her only child, you could say that I'm the sunshine in her day. Put simply, even at my age, I basically am her life.

Throughout my entire existence, my mom has been my loudest cheerleader, telling others about whatever I was involved in at that particular time. As an actor, as a writer, producing stuff, or even when I was back in college or grad school climbing the rungs as a therapist, she wanted people to know. It didn't matter if you cared or not, she wanted everyone to know how happy she was about her son. We're talking about people who had never met me, so I'm positive they had very little interest in hearing about it. In fact, I'm not convinced that some of them didn't run away when they saw her coming.

But God bless her, she's always loved me. At the end of the day, she's never cared what other people think of her stories about me. I'm her son, and she's proud of what I've done and who I am, and she's glad to tell anyone within earshot. While it can be a little embarrassing, I also realize it's very flattering, and I love her for it.

I could only imagine how devastated my mom would be to get blindsided by the news that I'd killed myself. So when I was pondering it, when I realized that kind of news might actually overwhelm her and kill her, I knew that I couldn't handle that. She didn't deserve that. She'd been so good to me and to the world.

My dad's reaction, while obviously not good, would have been more difficult to predict. He's always had this very strong, protective nature about him that seems to cover a sometimes-tortured soul. Perhaps he'd have just stuffed it down with the rest of the stuff he's dealt with in life. I don't know. What I do know is that dealing with the private hauntings of the past while also trying to maintain a strong, steady hand of gentle guidance in the present can be a tricky thing. Subsequently, he's always had a more difficult time juggling ideas while simultaneously processing or expressing his emotions. Obviously, whatever his reaction to my death, it would be devastating for him.

I just couldn't picture doing anything that might paralyze him from being able to continue living a peaceful life. And I know my dad. He'd have agonized over this forever in the silent pain and torture of not knowing how to express himself over it. I couldn't leave this world with that on my conscience.

Beyond my parents, I started realizing the spiritual consequences of killing myself.

Who wins in a battle of wills between man and God?

I feared that if I killed myself, I might be forced to wander the planet as a ghost for a number of untold years.

Since God exists not only in time but also outside of time, I questioned whether these unspecified years could morph into an eternal wandering on the earth, or even worse, the condemnation to stagger through a personally created Hell of loneliness and isolation from God and humanity forever.

That seemed like a horrific fate.

So there I was. I was in a mental hell already, but I had the spiritual component against me and the weight of pain that I'd cause my parents if I chose to kill myself.

Ultimately, another long-held belief that suicide is a selfish act, with no regard or love for the people left behind, really weighed on me too.

But with my friends and family, I couldn't be selfish. I loved my family. I loved my friends.

No matter how messed up I was, and no matter who found out about it or ridiculed me for being stupid, as long as my family was all right and my friends were okay, I had no option but to deal with this somehow. I didn't know how at the time, but there had to be some way.

It may have been some of the best, most rational thinking I'd done in months. Maybe it was just a lack of options to do anything else. Maybe it was just the lack of actually having a gun.

W HEN EIGHTY THOUSAND PEOPLE *are made redundant so quickly and can't find replacement jobs of the same or greater value, they are often forced to move elsewhere, and that's exactly what happened in Flint. When they moved, there were a lot fewer people. When there were fewer people, there were fewer property taxes going to the city to keep it beautiful, and housing values plummeted overnight. New people that previously couldn't have afforded to live there began to buy or rent, and that brought a lower class to Flint than had ever existed there before. When the social classes began to change, people in the higher classes left. Those in the middle class that could afford to move elsewhere also did so. Within three years, a mass exodus had taken place, and our beautiful city was infested with crime, looked like a war zone, and became filthy dirty. With a shrinking population and less tax revenue for the city, the place turned into a replica of South Central Los Angeles. The same thing happened in Detroit, and basically what was left was the image of Flint and Detroit that tattooed itself into the brains of people over the past thirty years.*

This was all quite traumatic to a little guy, and with my family falling apart, I was struggling to make sense of what was happening to my once stable life. People were frustrated in just about every way you could imagine, and something was suddenly happening that hadn't happened in our blue-collar community before: people were struggling financially.

My family now seemed to detest each other, and no one was talking. When they did, it was to yell about who was right and who was wrong. Now that my parents were divorced, my dad lived somewhere else, and Grandpa Goss had fallen entirely off the map. Uncle Dave and Uncle Mark had grown up and moved out, and their absence made Grandma Goss's house a target. One day, when Grandma Goss was visiting my mom and me (still living in our house fifteen miles away), three burglars ransacked her house and stole many of the sentimental items that had made that house a home. We were vulnerable for the first time in my life, and I was terrified of the dangers facing us, while our quality of life spiraled quickly downward and out of control.

My dad's job was still secure, but my mom, who'd given up her job to raise me, wasn't so lucky. With so many layoffs at GM, she couldn't get back in, and she was forced to take a much lower-paying job in a grocery store just to get by. This was at a time when good jobs for women were scarce, and the general attitude toward women in the workplace was much different than it is today. I became a latchkey kid at the age of eight and began taking care of myself at my mom's house when she worked, all the while wishing for some way to escape the unhappiness of it all.

It's no coincidence that Grandpa and Grandma Rice and the stability and familiarity their life in Chicago represented became more important to me around that time. Chicago had always wowed me, but now, it represented more. It still shined. It was an opportunity to grasp back at the good life we'd all had—only my grandparents were still living it there in the big city. Beyond that, their life represented the happiness that had previously been all through my family, and with them, there was still something to celebrate.

I loved Chicago. Every time I went to visit, I was captivated by everything in sight. Michigan Avenue, the Sears Tower, Water Tower Place, roller skating at the park, Shedd Aquarium, the museums, Navy Pier ... you name it.

When I got to the age that I could visit my grandparents alone, I was gone. The highlight of my summer vacations from school was having time to be in Chicago with Grandpa and Grandma Rice. I became fascinated with the place, and the decisions Grandpa Rice had made that rewarded him so well in life when so many others were coming to the end of their rainbows. I tried to drink in everything about him, whether it was his character or the slow, quiet way he thought things through and processed life. He was so unlike what all the stereotypes of success looked like. He was modest and honest and not at all interested in glorifying himself. He was, to put it simply, the antithesis of all that I'd seen and all the supposed images of success we still see today. And yet, even though he was completely unlike the common perception of success, he was by far the most successful man I knew. He never forgot where he came from, and even in his later years, while far more sophisticated than when he'd begun his life, he was at heart still the same "small-town boy" who'd grown up on his parents' farm. The only difference was that he was now that same guy and living near the top of the John Hancock Building. When he went swimming or to the health club, it was on the forty-fourth floor of the building. But it was the values he'd learned back on the farm in Michigan that had ultimately given him the life he was so blessed to have lived there in the Windy City.

I started going to Chicago every summer, and several other times during the year, when my dad would take me to see his parents. We did things like that to maintain some consistency and connection to what our life had been before the divorce. I'm sure my dad was aware of the trauma that losing Grandpa Goss had been to my life, and most likely, this was his way of preserving one little corner of my universe.

I learned about something else in Chicago that captivated me and cultivated my love of travel, trains, and cars. Just as I'd enjoyed when my dad had taken me to family day at Buick, I was intrigued by my grandpa's workplace, so at the end of the day, my grandma and I would walk to my grandpa's job so we could all walk home together.

My grandpa seemed to have a fancy person's job because people wore suits and ties at his office, but it didn't have the action my dad's did, with the cars rolling off the line and whatnot. I'm not exactly sure when I was told, but I learned that from Grandpa's window in the Federal Building, I could see a road called Route 66 that began just a few blocks away and didn't end until it got all the way to Santa Monica, California! I walked on that road on the way to meet Grandpa, and with my appreciation of maps and traveling the country, that was pretty impressive. Although I hadn't heard of it before, it seemed cool that a road that began in Chicago didn't end until California, and I imagined it must be one of the longest in the USA. At the time, I wasn't sure it was anything more impressive than I-75 back home, which was pretty long too. I was told Route 66 allowed all those cars from Flint to take people out to Hollywood, where they became famous and sought their fame and fortune. I was assured it was much more famous than I-75, and had been for a lot longer. And there it was, right next to Grandpa's workplace in Chicago. It seemed to me that Chicago wasn't just a mystical place ... it had the best of everything.

I needed something like that to hold on to, some piece of excellence that wasn't fading away. With the loss of Grandpa Goss, my grandparents' divorce, my parents' divorce, and the rapid dissolution of my original hometown of Flint, Michigan, all within the space of about three years, everything back there seemed in a shambles. I began to dread going back to it. All the crazy racial tensions, unemployment, anger toward the government, and the sexual revolution stuff had created an anxiety that didn't seem to exist when I was in Chicago with Grandpa and Grandma Rice. People there were accepting and friendly. The people I met all knew how to get along. It soothed me. I needed people to get along and be nice to one another. After my initial upbringing, having harmony between people was in my makeup.

From the sill of their corner-unit condo high in the John Hancock Building, I'd gaze out across the city after everyone had gone to sleep, and whatever turmoil was brewing inside my little heart seemed to calm itself. Far below, I could see all the cars on the different highways or heading up Lakeshore Drive to peaceful places beside Lake Michigan. I'd lie there and listen as the music of the traffic lulled me into a peaceful sleep, and once again, it was the cars and their travel to mysterious places that restored my contentment. Even when sirens would wail in the distance, from my perspective up above, I got a glimpse into the serenity of God. Down on the ground, a fire truck might race to a scene, but up there so high above it, the intensity of what they were experiencing had no immediacy. I understood God's larger view of it all. No need to panic. A larger view gave a calmer perspective. Across the city, there was mostly just beauty, and He had given me the ability to see it.

With that new "God-perspective," Chicago permanently marked itself on my heart and on my soul. Up there among the clouds, I felt like I'd found Heaven.

Sixteen

~

"Crossroads"

I needed to see Dr. Ludwig, to tell him what was happening with me.

He was very laid back about it, like a surgeon who has performed a particular surgery a thousand times. I told him I wasn't the suicidal type before all of this started, and he asked me what medication I was taking for depression. Once I told him, he calmly suggested that I stop the antidepressant I was on. He offered that some medications affect people differently, and just because one might not work, another just might. He also said that because of my panic attacks there was a specific medication he thought I should try. This one would not only handle my depression but also hopefully get my anxiety under control to stop those pesky panic attacks.

That would be heaven-sent, I thought. As soon as I got home, I ripped open the new prescription and started popping my new pills. No deep thought had to go into it this time. I'd already crossed that psychological barrier and left it in the dust. Heck, by now I was content ingesting the dust. I was committed to getting out of my mental state, whatever it took. I'd finally accepted that things were different now. I was different now.

The guy I remembered, with all his drive and personality, just wasn't me anymore. And if I was going to keep this new guy alive, I needed to put the protections in there to keep him that way. Whatever Dr. Ludwig said, whether he told me to hang upside down by my toenails, I was ready and willing to do it. I just couldn't let my brain get the better of me any longer. I wanted to find a way to live, and if I was going to do that, I needed to figure out a way to subdue it and do what I had to in order to flourish.

I'd been desperately grasping at straws to do something that could help me feel useful.

The only thing I had left that wasn't warped or distorted was my faith.

The most sustaining place I did feel I've fit throughout my life has often been with spiritual people who have a real faith in God and who show it in the ways they treat others as opposed to those individuals who claim to have a faith simply by showing up late for church.

I do serve in my church, but for me, it's always been about being close to people who really try to live their lives for God, regardless of whether or not they go to church. I know the Bible says to "not forsake the gathering," but I'm talking about people whose faith is in their hearts, and in their minds, and who live their lives in the most moral, loving way toward themselves and others that they can. All too often, I just haven't found these people in church. I'm not trying to sound "anti-church," because I'm not. It's just that I haven't had the best experiences of finding the most loving people there.

Shortly before the accident, I'd begun attending a new church. In the wake of my depression and helplessness, there was one thing I knew to be true: my faith was something I could still have and practice despite the difficulties of my injury, so I'd decided to invest myself in church again. I found what I thought was a good church nearby and involved myself as I had in my twenties, hoping to find something that would give me a little direction and some sort of usefulness through my injury.

One day, the church had some people come in to talk about a summer camp for abused kids, a place called Royal Family Kids' Camp. It was an outside organization—a sort of local missions organization. They needed volunteers to come forward as unpaid counselors, people who were willing to work with abused, neglected, and abandoned kids who might be at risk for one day going into the probation or legal system, or any troubled kid who might end up being there. Might I be willing to help?

Despite my nervousness, I agreed. Our staff traveled up to the mountains in Big Bear, California, and the day the kids got there, something clicked in me—something that hadn't been affected by the accident. Whatever I'd inherited from my dad over the years, that ability to be strong and protective, while gently guiding and firm ... it was there and it was intact. I did have some mental struggles going on, but they didn't really impact my ability to be a surrogate dad to these boys for the week. It was as if God had chosen the perfect kids for me.

One of the boys I was given was a nine-year-old named Gary.

I thought I might be in trouble at first, because, as it turned out, Gary was a practical joker. As soon as the kids got off the bus, I started looking for him. The camp didn't want any kid arriving and feeling lost or like they had no one waiting for them, so the whole group of counselors and staff gathered at the bus, excitedly greeting the kids as they arrived.

I found my first child camper easily ... in fact, he already knew my name and came to find me. But one kid was standing there looking at me, and when I asked if he was Gary, he said, "No, I'm Darnell," and darted off. Okay, I thought. I needed to keep searching.

And I did. I searched. And I searched.

Meanwhile "Darnell" was terrorizing some of the girls, pushing some of the boys, and raising a fuss with pretty much everyone in sight.

I'm glad that's not my kid, I thought.

The longer I stood there fielding the crowd for Gary, the more the number of kids dwindled. I'd watch as the counselors and kids met and ran off to see their rooms, while "Darnell" was still causing a ruckus. It started to become clear.

Darnell was Gary.

Finally, the jig was up. I approached "Darnell" and asked, "Are you Gary?"

"No, I'm Darnell," he responded with all the convincing ability he could muster.

"Well, let's go 'Darnell' ... I can't have you running off here without a counselor. I'll just keep you until Gary shows up."

Hmm. He eyed me suspiciously. How could he get out of this?

I noticed about that time that the name tag around his neck had been turned backward. I reached out for it and turned it around.

"Well, what do you know? ... Gary!"

"I stole it from him," he replied.

Oh, man. It was going to be a long week.

Seventeen

~

GARY LIKED TO CAUSE TROUBLE, and I was more than happy to enforce consequences. We spent a lot of time in "time out," specifically one time after he'd tried to kill a gray squirrel with a rock. I was extremely firm on this one, and we went directly to time out.

Many of the other counselors frowned on me for doing this. At one point, three of them ganged up to tell me how this was supposed to be a week of fun for these kids, and how I was being inappropriate by being so tough on Gary. They felt we weren't going to make any lasting changes with these kids because once the week was over, we weren't allowed to have contact with them again. They wanted me to ease up and let Gary have fun, however he wanted to have it, and whether I agreed with it or not.

There were three of them. One of me. I was outnumbered.

With Gary standing beside me, surely desperate that I'd listen to their pleas on his behalf for mayhem, dumb, old brain-damaged Dan decided to take a stand against all three of these "normal-minded" guys. I told them how inappropriate I thought it was that they'd condone Gary killing the squirrel, and how they were letting their kids act like wild animals in the name of fun.

"You know, this might be my only week ever with Gary. And you can let your boys kill things, hit each other, and scream, and do whatever you want …"

Gary looked up at me. There was a "but" coming.

"… but Gary is my boy, and my boy is going to learn what it means to be a gentleman. My boy's going to know that he's got someone who not only cares about him but also has expectations for him and his behavior."

The other counselors looked at me with disdain, but I noticed that Gary's little nine-year-old eyes lit up when I'd used the words "Gary" and "my boy" in the same sentence—like he was hearing words he'd never heard before. This "Dan," who only a few days before had been a stranger, was actually taking ownership of him like he mattered. A minute before, he probably wasn't sure this "mean old guy" even liked him.

His eyes never left me.

"I want Gary's life to go well. I'm going to teach him in five days everything I can about how to make it go that way. And once we get out of here, your kids will go back to acting like animals, but my boy is going to remember me. And he's going to know he has a chance out of the life he has if he just keeps doing what I tell him here."

Well, the other counselors sort of threw up their hands in defeat. Clearly, they thought I wasn't "getting it." They walked away, and I know that one of them that had been particularly critical of me started telling people I had "something wrong" with me.

People thinking that was usually my biggest fear. But for some reason, it didn't bother me at all now because I knew in my heart that something was happening that was completely right between Gary and me. Something broke in that very moment for the two of us. Gone was his defiance toward me. Sure, he still had his tough little independent guy attitude. But with me, from that point forward, he was calm. In fact, I was the only one he'd calm down for. By the end of that third night, his toughness with me was completely gone, replaced by a playfulness that only a kid can muster. We played chase outside, just him and me, and he marveled that he could "juke" past me without me catching him. Of course, I didn't try too hard. I wanted him to feel that he could spread his wings and do things that only he could do. I wanted him to know that he had a value all his own.

On the last morning of camp, we sat looking out at the crowd of kids, and he leaned his head against my arm. He took my big white hand in his little black one, and he looked at them side by side. Then he just grabbed my hand and held it.

I didn't know how this kid had managed to restore my feeling of worth in the world, but he had.

When it was time for the kids to board the bus, Gary and I were pretty quiet. I'd told him earlier that morning, "Gary, you've got a good sense of humor, and you know what that means?"

He didn't.

I told him it meant he was really, really smart. He looked at me like he'd never thought of that before. He didn't do that well in school.

It didn't matter. I explained, "A lot of people are smart, but not all smart people are funny. It takes a lot of smarts to know how to make people laugh. You're a smart boy, and you have a good heart. You have a presence that people are drawn to, and I want you to listen to this: you're going to have to learn how to use your presence. If you use the attention that comes your way for bad things, you're going to quickly get the wrong people around you, and you will not have the good life I know you can have. Or you can use it for good, and I promise that your life will turn out happier than you can imagine right now. I want you to always remember this. You have the power to choose the life you will have. Just choose 'good.'"

He told me that morning he would.

Gary had shaken me up. He'd helped me feel useful again, as if I had something to contribute to the world, something I hadn't felt in a long, long time. I'd been down before I got to camp, but being there, being focused on someone other than myself, someone who was dependent on me being able to take good care of him had shifted my focus outward, and it felt good. It made me realize I needed to keep focused on others. It was obvious to everyone I was dealing with more than just saying good-bye to Gary, so when it came to my time to share, I stood up and came out with it publicly: how I was suffering from a brain injury, and how tough the last year had been. How I'd doubted myself and my ability to keep going on.

I shared how I'd not felt any value before this week, and how Gary had given it back to me. I thanked them all for giving me the opportunity to be there and to have this feeling again. Like I mattered.

Later that Friday night, one of the associate directors of the camp, a man named Kenny, told me that he and the director, an amazingly big-hearted woman named Deanna Wilcox, had prayed beforehand for each child when they were matching up kids with counselors. Deanna wasn't only thorough, she was spiritually insightful. She'd wanted to make sure God gave each child exactly who they needed. What I realized was that she and Kenny had also been praying for me. My match with Gary was no coincidence. God still had me on His highway, and somehow, I was exactly where I was supposed to be.

*B*Y 1983, I was at an age where a boy needs his dad more, and I'd moved from my mom's home to my dad's. For the next five years, my dad began to school me in the economics of what was happening around me. The auto industry was next to dead in Flint, and the city had become a cesspool. While GM was declaring losses on the news each night and laying off more people all the time, I couldn't understand how they were still posting record profits. How could they be making so much money but put it in the news that they were losing so much that they had to continue laying people off?

What no one seemed to understand was that the losses they claimed in the news were against projected earnings for the year. When they didn't make those forecasted earnings, they declared a loss, which meant there was no more profit sharing for employees, and there was no more hiring. It didn't mean they weren't making money, it just meant they weren't claiming it, and by declaring losses, they could save themselves from paying bonuses to the people who were helping them make the money that was still rolling in. Basically, they were getting greedy and putting the screws to people who'd helped them become the largest company in the world, and who now had no recourse. Meanwhile, GM was spending billions to develop robots that would automate their line and that, over the long term, would mean those jobs they'd taken from people would stay gone.

It was probably an oversight on their part, but the psychological impression GM was making on my generation was that they were a bunch of losers. They were sending the message that they couldn't put out a profitable product. Meanwhile, the new foreign car companies were capitalizing on that by promoting how unreliable the American cars were when compared with theirs, while also marketing their exciting new and, most important, less expensive models. In Michigan, it was still taboo to conceive of buying a foreign car, but I knew that among my friends, boys were now talking about Porsches, BMWs, Mercedes, Lexus, and many other foreign models instead of the old standby Chevys and Fords. For all the luxury GM probably still thought they were offering, I'm positive I never heard anyone say they wanted a Cadillac when they got old enough to buy one. In 1984, a new Corvette was introduced, and that got everybody temporarily excited, except that GM had run up the price so high that none of the rank-and-file guys could afford one. This was a serious error on GM's part *because the blue-collar guys had been the core buyers who had popularized the car. This didn't really hurt any of the blue-collar fans, however, because the secret soon got out that the '84 Vette was junk. Suddenly, the true fans had saved their money, and GM had succeeded in making themselves look incompetent of producing anything good, even their flagship sports car. The stage was set for the foreign car companies to go wild with their message of superior quality, and GM had virtually guaranteed it for them.*

Uncle Mark did something that mortified the whole family. When he'd gone to GM and tried to hire in, they'd rejected him, so, in anger, he bought a Honda as revenge. While it didn't make sense to us why he'd strengthen a foreign car line when his family was struggling to hold onto the few GM jobs that were left, I have to guess that he wasn't the only one across the country feeling that way, because the foreign car companies started growing by leaps and bounds in the '80s.

On the West Coast, foreign cars were selling like hotcakes. In a place where what's new is always what's in style—whether or not it's actually good for you—the foreign car companies started growing roots. The deeper those roots went, the more American water was sucked out of the Midwestern soil, and the USA got weaker while Japan got stronger.

I remember my dad relaying a story to me that he couldn't understand: how when, just forty years before in World War II, some of the Japanese had practiced actually eating their prisoners of war, our country was now buying cars from them. I guess it was ironic, then, that some Americans were now going hungry. When the Yugo came out, he explained to me how shell casings on artillery used by the Vietcong in Vietnam had been found and discovered to have come out of Yugoslavia. Now, even though Yugoslavia had helped kill Americans just ten years before by supplying artillery to Vietnam, Americans were rewarding them by buying Yugos.

Fortunately, nobody ever said, "Those Yugoslavians sure can build a great car!" and before long, they were out of business. Unfortunately, the economic climate was set for whatever foreign car would come in to replace it on the market.

One thing that amazed me was that even though my dad still had a great job, he still cared so much about his friends who'd been put out of work over the years. He seemed like an attorney advocating for a jilted wife in a marriage where the husband, in this case GM, had cheated on her repeatedly while she'd stayed steadfast beside him. More amazing to me was that while he understood but disagreed with the business moves GM was making, he continued to go to work loyally and do the best job he could do for them. He never considered for one moment that we weren't a GM family, and he continued to buy all our cars from them. At the same time, he never looked away from the bodies left behind. One thing I learned about my dad was that whether he agreed with you or not, he'd stand by you. Obviously, he didn't agree with how GM was treating its employees, especially because he was one of them. Although he knew the profits were high, creative accounting was allowing the higher-ups to neglect rewarding the little guys who had helped build the company. At the same time, my dad made it very clear to me that a purchase against GM meant a purchase against the guys who built the cars, and if we wanted to keep our money in our economy, we had to keep buying American. Basic economics taught that demand for products would mean more supply was created, and creating that supply meant workers were needed to create those products. As long as my dad kept buying American, he was doing his part to keep the demand for American cars up, and that meant American workers would have to stay in the factories to build them. My dad wanted to make sure those guys on the line kept their jobs, kept working, and continued to feed their families.

He didn't stop at just advocating for buying American cars. My dad began promoting the idea of buying everything American, because if you bought American TVs, American clothes, even American beer, it kept those American companies in business. Every purchase of a foreign product meant another dollar taken away from our American companies, and as I watched the economy crumbling around me, everything he said was almost immediately borne out in the economic landscape I saw.

Eighteen

~

"In the Midnight Hour"

SOMETHING HAD SHIFTED IN ME significantly. I was coming off the high of having been so adept at working productively and feeling so normal at camp that I needed to do whatever I could to keep it going. That's probably what motivated me to think back to Lisa, the girl I'd talked to at the brain injury rehab place all those months before.

She'd been so sweet with me, and it was clear she'd wanted to help. At that time, I just wasn't ready to admit I was brain-damaged, but I'd admitted that to myself now. Maybe coming off the success of being with Gary at camp, I'd gotten the sign that being brain-injured wasn't necessarily a death sentence. If there was a way of improving myself, I needed to look into it.

I called Lisa and reintroduced myself. She seemed to remember me and was very simple and to the point. She'd set an appointment for me to come and see her facility.

I was nervous, but I agreed. She sounded excited to meet me, like this was going to be easy. All I had to do was show up, and my life would get better. That's truly the vibe she put out. Just show up. That's all I had to do.

That's easier said than done. I anguished for the next few days, regressing to earlier thoughts of not wanting to be diagnosed as needing rehab. I tried to tell myself I was on the mend and should cancel, but after all I'd been through, I knew better. All I allowed myself to do was be tempted by canceling. I knew in my heart that it'd be a dumb thing to do, so I put it out of my mind. Still, this inner turmoil bothered me. Why was I still fighting this?

I guess maybe because after the success I'd had at camp, I didn't want to go to rehab and get relabeled as deficient. I'd only just started feeling sort of normal, and I was in no rush to let go of it. I argued with myself.

I'm deficient! No, I'm not! I'm deficient! No, I'm not. After all, I'd been great at camp. How could anyone say I was deficient? The truth is, I needed to face it, whether people said so or not.

So on that Tuesday, I did. I showed up and met a girl named Amy at the front desk, who shortly thereafter introduced me to Lisa.

Lisa was very cute, tiny, and maybe five to ten years older than me. Along with her co-workers, Roslyn and Craig, we exchanged nervous pleasantries in the lobby of the place. It was far from what I'd expected, with a nice carpet on the floor, soothing artwork, and fancy furniture all around. The three of them took me to a large conference room with an extremely long table surrounded by plush chairs. I instantly felt like I was in a job interview. Did I have to prove how "crazy" I was to be accepted here? I glanced up at the three of them across from me.

This guy, Craig, really unnerved me, and it was strange as to why. With his short hair parted to the side and his perfect presentation, he was a vision of me ten years earlier. Granted, he was a little older than me, but I looked at him and knew we'd had very similar experiences. Back then, I'd been through grad school and was working in private practice. I imagined he'd been cutting his teeth somewhere else around the same time. I was very intellectual and academic, affable, and extremely straitlaced with a tie and polished shoes every day. As I sat staring at him, he was pretty much the picture of that now.

It was just unsettling. Seeing him represented what I could have been.
But I was damaged, and the fact that I was here meant they all knew it.

I became extremely self-conscious. Had I not been in an accident, Craig could have been a peer or co-worker. We'd have been friends, probably. Now, I was sure he'd look at me as just another patient.

I knew we'd never be friends because he just wouldn't have allowed it. I wasn't in his crowd. Just as I'd done when my old patients took drugs to be normal, he'd look down on me. I was convinced that Craig, despite his affable smile, was making an unconscious mental judgment on me even as we sat across from each other. Realizing that he'd never allow us to become friends, I was convinced that from there on out, our roads in life had diverged. There was what he was and there was what I'd become.

Simple enough. I was now a patient, and I needed drugs to be normal.
I squirmed in my seat as the three of them talked to me—Craig, Roslyn, and Lisa. I wanted to bolt from the chair to get away from Craig. Not that he ever gave me any clue that the story I'd created for him had one iota of substance. He hadn't, but I was convinced of it, and it took everything I had not to get up and leave. I didn't want to be reminded of what I'd been, and looking at him drove that point home clearer than anything I could have imagined.

It was my boy Gary that kept me sitting there. No, he wasn't there with me physically, but he was there in my memory, and my memories of camp told me who I could be in the full-time future if I just stay seated. I needed to get back to being competent like I'd been with Gary. I couldn't continue as I had before ... suicidal and angry, suffering from panic attacks at any hour of the day or night.

I'm not sure I really heard anything the three of them said to me. Maybe I answered questions, I don't remember. I just know I felt as if some sort of surreal haze had descended around me. I was becoming over-whelmed again and wondering how on earth a guy like me could end up here. What if people found out I was in treatment for a brain injury? Would they call me crazy? I needed to keep this quiet.

About that time, I started hearing someone hooting and hollering down the hallway. What I expected was to see a lot of people who'd lost control of their faculties or impulse controls screaming out or crying the way you see in a lot of nursing homes.

As I left the conference room with Lisa, Craig, and Roslyn, Roslyn started to chuckle about all the hooting and hollering going on.

"That Tony ..." she said, clearly tickled.

Tony? I wondered. Who was Tony?

Working down the hall stood this tall Latin guy, his hands moving in hugely animated gestures for the patients sitting near him, their laughter keeping him company. He was raising a ruckus of hilarity to buoy the spir-its of the patients.

That's when Roslyn tacked something on to her statement that just about floored me.

"We need more clients like him. He's such a character!"

Tony was a patient? I'd been fooled! I couldn't tell the difference between him and the staff. He looked normal, but he was brain-damaged, just like me.

Then I stopped to correct myself. He wasn't like me at all.

The guy's attitude was great, and I could tell he made all his peers feel just a little better about their lot in life. If he could be this good, this alive, then maybe they could too. Heck, maybe I could. He brought hope to everyone right there.

I realized that I'd been so backward about my situation. I'd been so down and negative. So ashamed. My attitude had been all wrong, and there was no way I was going to be able to get back to the world with the atti-tude I had. I needed to change things up if I wanted that.

But here I was, looking at Tony. I was looking at my new role mod-el. I needed to be just like him, even if I didn't completely believe I could be.

I stood there in the hallway transfixed by the guy, this peer, this partner in my suffering. All I saw was joy and fun in him. How did he get like that?

Suddenly, I got snapped out of my trance. Tony was staring right over at me, smiling. "Hey, bro!" he called.

I looked around. He was still looking right at me. Obviously, he didn't know me, but was he actually talking to me?

"How you doin', bro?" he called again. He kept looking right at me, expectantly, a friendly smile on his face, my welcome to the facility, so to speak.

"Good," I said, unable to manage anything more.

"Good deal, bro," he threw back.

Had I just made my first friend? I guess so. And you'd have thought I'd met Babe Ruth. This guy was a champion to the other injured patients—you could see that. I determined that where he was then was exactly where I needed to be.

Tony had turned back to one of the other patients, and I turned back to Lisa. She had plans to get me started on my own treatment.

"When do you want to start?" she asked.

If it meant I'd end up like Tony, it couldn't be soon enough.

Nineteen

~

"Mercy, Mercy Me"

LISA ASKED ME TO COME IN when I had a few days to spend in testing. I'd take a battery of tests to determine the extent of my brain damage, and then a course of treatment would be set to deal with the trouble spots. I started feeling a bit like a lab rat.

Tammy was introduced to me on my first testing day. She was a speech therapist, and she was as calm and nurturing as anyone I'd met in quite a long time, and that helped settle me a bit. As she gave me one neurological test after another, I could tell she was an extremely pleasant person. Tall and kind, like a graceful willow tree in the wind, I could see from the level of compassion she exuded that she felt a lot of empathy for my situation. Never at any time did it seem like she looked down on me or saw me as anything less than anyone else. That meant a lot to me because as someone who was simply dealing with a condition, it made me believe I might be able to get to a point where I could leave this condition behind and be equal to others again.

At the end of the testing, the results weren't good. I had problems in a lot of different parts of my brain. I'd been hit in the front hard enough to bounce my brain off the back of my skull, so there was damage back there too. I was told that all the medial connections between the front and back of my brain had been affected because of this. I had a lot of work to do.

The test results revealed a myriad of weird things, some of which I already knew. Among other things, I had problems with my ability to process information and with my long- and short-term memory. I couldn't read anymore, but I could write a sentence fine. Don't ask me to read it to you afterward, but, hey, I could write it. The thing that blew me away was that even though I couldn't understand a lot of what people might say to me, my vocabulary still tested off the charts! I could talk to you using big words, write elaborately constructed letters, and type sixty-five words per minute, which looks really good to the outside world. Unfortunately, I couldn't tell you what any of those same big words meant, and I couldn't read what any of those elaborate letters said. Bizarre. But because I'd appeared so normal to so many people, I'd been able to hide undetected for so long, even as I descended to the point of considering my own suicide. Had it not been for Billy Brown, Tracy Baer, and Dr. Ludwig, I'd have slid along even further. It only takes one person to make a difference.

On my first day of actual rehab, I sat with a new girl, also named Amy, in the Occupational Therapy room, or OT, as we called it.

Amy2 was assigned to check out the alignment of my eyes. I'd started having double vision in combination with massive headaches. It wasn't constant but usually happened if I got tired or stressed, and I'd end up looking like Marty Feldman. Amy2 did a visual test with me that involved some simple string and some very average beads. She asked me to line up the beads in my vision so I could see them in a certain pattern combined with the string.

I was unable to do it, and I knew instantly by her look that I'd been caught. All those months of trying to fake people out, and in my very first test here, Amy2 had broken through my façade in about ten seconds. Now someone who had not directly been told about my problems not only knew I had them, she also had measurable proof and knew way more about them than I wanted her to.

For some reason, that overwhelmed me. It was only my first test that day. How much more were they going to find wrong with me? Who was I now? How much work did I have in front of me? Was I in over my head? I was afraid to find out—petrified, even.

I burst into tears like a kindergarten-age girl, and I was immediately embarrassed by it. This had been building up for a long time, and I guess the dam simply broke. Rather than wait for me to toughen up and get mad about the "stupidity" of my behavior, Amy2 put her hand on my shoulder.

"Do you want me to give you a minute?" she asked.

I did, and she left for the briefest of instants. When she returned, I'd composed myself and apologized. I explained that it was hard to admit I was affected by this traumatic brain injury, or "TBI," as Tammy the speech therapist had called it.

Technically, I'd been told I had an "MTBI," or mild traumatic brain injury. That was almost laughable. This was mild?

All those months of decline were mild?

Considering suicide was mild?

Regardless, Amy2 and I worked for a bit that day, and for my trouble, I was awarded my very own string and sight beads to work with at home. It seemed that my headaches and dizziness had been caused by a specific type of damage to my brain that had given me the double vision in the first place. So it was possible that I wasn't getting double vision because of my migraines, but just the opposite.

After seeing Amy2, I went to Mike, the physical therapist, in the next room over. This was the first place I experienced success in rehab. He did a bunch of tests on my strength and balance, but, as you may remember, I'd continued working out after my accident, on the advice of my chiropractor. With no job, and nothing to do but hit the gym, I was actually in some of the best physical shape of my life.

Mike would throw an exercise at me, and I'd sail through it with flying colors. Another one, and it'd be the same result. Following my chiropractor's advice all those months back meant that there was one less thing I needed to focus on in my recovery.

Mike cut me loose from physical therapy after my first week there. Whatever I'd been doing, he told me to keep doing. I'd passed his tests by a mile, and it felt good.

What I'd sailed through with Mike, however, was more than made up for by all that I struggled to get through with my speech therapist, Tammy. She worked on way more than speech. In fact, she worked on everything else in my brain that needed working on. You name it, she did it.

I had to remember three numbers. That's it. Just three numbers. I'd sit in front of her computer and numbers would flash. When they were finished, I'd have five seconds to remember and click them on her screen.

I failed miserably. For weeks, I worked on remembering those three numbers until finally I got it and was able to move on to that magic number "four." That was a big moment for me.

All my exercises started small and were timed. They seemed simple to the average passerby, but because of my original assessment, Tammy knew exactly where I was and where to start me.

As it turns out, I'd had more damage than I had been aware of. When I finished the original testing and was told about my "M" TBI, I'd gone back to see Dr. Ludwig. He'd been the one who explained the point I made earlier, that when I was hit in the accident, the truck tire hit me so hard that my brain bounced around in my skull to damage the front and the back of it. That's called a "contra-coup" injury. The corresponding connections in the medial (or middle) part of my brain had been scrambled too. In short, my entire brain was experiencing some sort of trouble, and until I worked on exercises specific to fixing each portion of it, I was going to have problems.

I saw my new friend Tony again during my first week, too, and while I definitely wasn't really feeling it, I was quick to show him the same amount of enthusiasm he'd shown to me before. He yelled his high-energy "How you doin', bro?" and I gave him a huge "Wassssssuuuuuppppp?!" which made him and the others around him laugh. He threw it right back at me, and due to his sheer volume, a lot of staff members started popping their heads out of their offices to see if everything was all right. Had someone just blown a gasket? As out-of-character for the place as it was for a couple of brain-damaged dudes to seem so deliriously happy to see each other, I think it was nice to have good vibes flowing between the patients.

Tony seemed happy to have a partner in crime, and he'd push me along whether I felt like it or not. We'd build a two-man pep rally each morning in the large Occupational Therapy room, and the energy we generated was appreciated by not only the other patients but also by the staff. In fact, it was as if the staff enjoyed it even more. There was a sense of awe that two injured dudes could work up a crowd into such positive feelings in the middle of a rehab. We weren't trying to be showboats or draw attention to ourselves; it was just bonding time between "injured folk." Spreading positive energy to the other patients was a temporary respite from the mental darkness.

By the way the staff treated us, you'd have thought we were all just dealing with a common cold. They basically treated us like we were additions to the staff, with our own jobs to do and no different from any of them. There didn't seem to be anyone who was treated like a patient, actually. That felt good, because at least for me, there was no sense I didn't fit in. In fact, I began to see that I fit in really well.

Amy, the front desk girl, often made flirty, funny comments to me, teasing me about something harmless but clearly set up to be at my expense. I'd come in and she'd make some disparaging comment like "Oh, no ... you again?" with a flirty smile. I'd come back at her with something like "That's right, baby ... now your day can start!" She'd roll her eyes, and whatever we'd do, there was a sense of fun I hadn't experienced in a long time. Suddenly, I wasn't the "drain" I'd felt like for most of the past year. I realized I was gaining a sense of worth again.

In a very short time, I went from being a completely depressed guy who lay in his bed all day to being the class clown at rehab. If there was someone I could find to have a laugh with, or get others to laugh at, I'd find them. Never in mean-spirited way, mind you, just something to laugh at life about, increase the sense of team togetherness, and decrease the sense of despair that can easily overtake a place filled with people lost in the muddled gray of our minds.

To my surprise, things were extremely easy to keep lighthearted there. I hadn't expected that in a place with so much high-stakes stuff going on. All of us patients were fighting for our lives in the sense that we were laboring hard to get them back.

I found myself wishing I'd gotten my head out of the sand much earlier. Why hadn't I?

*I*N LESS THAN EIGHTY YEARS, *our country had come through the Industrial Revolution as the world's giant of manufacturing, and suddenly, we'd lost our crown, and all those same manufacturing jobs were being done in other countries. That meant a lot of Americans were out of work.*

The Japanese car companies had been brilliant, too, because when Americans refused to buy foreign cars, the Japanese devised an ingenious scheme to "take care of us" by building auto plants here that would get Americans "back to work." Nobody seemed to realize that by creating and finding purchasers for all these foreign products, the foreign companies had stolen market share from the U.S. companies and put us "out of work" in the first place. Actually, that may be unfair to them because by buying their products, we'd really done it to ourselves.

It didn't matter. Desperate for employment, and with no crash economics courses forthcoming, Americans ate up the Japanese offers of new jobs, and before long, they were working for the companies that were slowly bleeding the money out of our economy. Meanwhile, these foreign car companies were getting very bold and aggressive in the placement of their plants. I remember when a Mazda plant was built in Flat Rock, Michigan. This was Michigan, for goodness' sake, the car capital of the world! But it was brilliant strategy on their part because they knew if they could soften the hard-line stance people took against them in a place like Michigan and actually get people there buying their cars, it wouldn't be long until the rest of the country was buying them too. And they were right. The systematic deconstruction of General Motors, the American auto industry, and American manufacturing in general had begun. It wouldn't be long before the patriotic loyalty of the American consumer would be swept away as well.

The funny part was that General Motors didn't seem to care, and their constant "woe is me" story while making big profits didn't seem to wash. When your company is in supposed chaos, you'd think there would be fewer trips to the country clubs, but that wasn't the case. There was no slow-down in the celebrations for GM's top brass. It was almost as if they were enjoying their "decline."

Reaganomics continued in full force, and the whole "trickle-down" theory that had been proposed seemed like a big joke in Michigan. I'm not sure where things were supposed to be trickling down to, but everything around Flint and Detroit was pretty dry. While the news showed the gala balls being held in Washington, Flint's unemployment rate inched upward toward 20 percent. Thank God my dad's job held strong.

In the early '80s, Grandpa Rice had earned the right to let go of his job and he retired from the Department of Labor in Chicago. During the winters, he'd grab my grandma and head somewhere warm to hit golf balls for a few months. They traveled to many places after he retired, such as Hawaii or the Gulf of Mexico in Gulf Shores, Alabama, but in 1985, he and my grandma decided to winter in New Mexico. My dad said we could drive out and see them over my Christmas break from school. I'd never been out West before, so just the idea was exciting. The American West! It felt so cool. I'd just gotten my driver's permit, too, so finally, my dad wouldn't do all the driving. One of the cool bonuses was that I'd finally get to travel on Route 66, that old road that ran past Grandpa's workplace in Chicago. The road had been decommissioned that same year with the completion of the Federal Highway System, but it was still there, minus the road signs. Anyhow, with my dad guiding the way, we'd get to drive on it for my own first cross-country drive.

On this trip, it was just going to be my dad and me, which seemed pretty cool. It was always interesting when it was just the two of us. When he was in parent mode, the dude was as hard-line and "on you" as you could imagine. He had strict expectations on conduct and right and wrong, and he taught extreme self-discipline. He was a good man, but if you deviated from what he was looking for in you, whoa … look out.

As I got older, some of the things he'd taught were starting to catch on and ingrain themselves, and he was in that "drill-instructor" mode less and less. He started to become my friend in addition to being my dad, and I think it was around this time I started to see the softness and gentle nature underneath his tough, farm-hewn exterior. I noticed that the quality of my life and my ability to take care of myself when compared to my peers was markedly advanced because of the many values and abilities I'd learned from my dad. That worked well for me because I knew from the loss of Grandpa Goss while in single digits that the only person who would ever truly be capable of helping me get my needs met outside of God Himself would be me. My dad's example and his instruction as a dad had helped me start heading in the right direction of self-sufficiency and provision.

One of the most powerful things my dad ever showed me in life was his work ethic. He'd worked hard for what we had, and he wasn't afraid to take on more if times called for it. The more I saw this "never quit" and "never give up" part of him, the less I resented what I'd often thought of as him being "mean" for pushing me so hard, and I realized he'd kept me on the straight and narrow when many of my peers went off the rails.

Don't get me wrong, I was no innocent. I got into trouble like most teenage boys, but the ever-present influence of my dad on my life, even when he was nowhere around, prevented me from getting too far off-track.

Although I often missed the huge party of people that was around me as a small boy with my mom's family, spending my teenage years with primarily just my dad was a pretty special experience.

Although I'd been taught to express my love for my family from an early age, I found it sad that Dad never talked much about his own up-bringing. It indicated a somewhat less than happy past.

I knew it had not always been a great childhood for him because Grandpa and Grandma Rice, despite how good they'd been to me, had grown up in a much different time, and they were very old-school in how they'd parented. They'd grown up as farmers during the Great Depression, and they'd figured out the secret to surviving. Basically, you'd better be willing to work like crazy to keep the wolves away from your door and never stop, in case the wolves ever returned. With that mindset, owning a farm and having two young boys worked right into their plans of surviving and thriving.

Twenty

~

"Any Day Now"

T AMMY HAD ME FOCUSED ON improving my processing speeds, my memory, and eventually relearning how to read, because my comprehension was shot. Because I'd lost all my sports knowledge, we thought maybe I could find some sports basics to read about, but I found that without having a ball in my hand or actually being on a field or court, the grueling chore of reading about sports was about as much fun as getting a taste of something by licking a "scratch-n'-sniff" sticker—not much joy in it. I couldn't get engrossed in sports anymore than I could in reading about a videogame. You've got to play it to actually enjoy, experience, and understand it.

Still, I didn't know if I was ready for that, so we came up with the idea to pick up some videogames of the sports I was trying to learn, which might make relearning them easier. However, because I didn't know the basic rules of the sports videogames I was trying to play, that fell flat. The games tended to move so fast I'd get destroyed and be out before I knew it. I got burnt out on all these games so fast that I questioned what I'd liked about sports in the first place.

Baseball, which had been one of my favorites, seemed awfully slow and long. It was like agony sitting there waiting for something to happen, and when something did, it only lasted about half a second.

Basketball, though tough to learn, was fast-paced and extremely physical, so I found that fun to watch. I wasn't sure if I could ever play it again because I didn't really comprehend all the rules anymore, but watching it was fun nonetheless. I told myself, just keep watching it, and I would learn it again. That didn't happen, though, without my coach or Dad sitting there explaining it to me like I was an eight-year-old.

It makes sense that kids start learning sports so young. They get a rudimentary amount of knowledge to be functional in the game their first year and then build upon that knowledge each subsequent year. Over the course of ten years, a person can become quite adept at something, but trying to learn all that information in just one year without a coach or a dad to explain it makes learning all these things more of a chore than fun. I started to get frustrated by sports. Here I was, with an extremely athletic body, and yet, actually trying to play anything seemed like a useless way of spending my time because I just wasn't getting it.

Football? Another favorite I'd once played. Forget it. Too many positions and different things going on. My understanding of it had vanished.

I resigned myself to the fact that unless I got an opportunity to actually play these games again, trying to pick them up was somewhat futile. I thought maybe getting out on the field in the practical play of the game would be a lot more instructional. In the meantime, I should let my frustrations go and concentrate for the time being on relearning things that could actually help me in the short term—things like reading.

I'm not sure Tammy even really cared if I relearned sports at all, but she was brilliant at finding something to get me turning the pages. The frustration in doing it was a different problem, but I'd been frustrated for a year anyway. Now I was frustrated, but I was regaining my reading skills at the same time. Instead of lose-lose, she'd already improved me 50 percent in this regard by turning it into a lose-win proposition.

Each day I'd come in and read something light. People magazine or something like that, but nothing that actually required any hard thinking. The girls in the office, Amy at the front desk in particular, would joke with me about reading all the office's gossip magazines, but I didn't care. I knew they were really supporting what I was doing to try to get better. Who cared if it was fluff?

It didn't stop there either. Once I started getting a little ways with it, I kept it going. I'd stop off at the grocery store, and I'd read anything that grabbed my interest. I'd get near the checkout lines and see what they had. Of all things, one of my favorite fluff things to read ended up being Soap Opera Digest.

Processing information and processing speed were both difficult for me. Tammy had gone through a whole laundry list of things for us to work on together, and over the months, we slowly started making it through. So I kept pushing and pushing. And with each day that I was in rehab, I not only saw the results in my performance, I could actually feel the difference in my brain.

At one point in my life, I'd gotten certified as a personal trainer, and one of my teachers made the analogy about training unused muscles. Often in the beginning, you see huge differences as a body is shocked into responding to the new strains put upon it. The initial gain and progress of strength is incredible.

The brain is no different. Just getting my brain engaged again, and in so many different ways, I could literally feel my mental sharpness being honed. I could see the difference between me and the person going through their ritualistic day-to-day activities without much thought. Basically, like a knife that was once sharp, these people get "dulled" by the same routines every day. Without regular sharpening, things start to wear down.

I was working on sharpening parts of my brain that I'd most likely not used in years. It was odd because even with brain damage, I started seeing an ability to outperform able-brained people in some regards. For that reason, I'm a big advocate of everybody doing some brainwork on a regular basis. I don't think there's a person alive who couldn't benefit from doing neuro-rehab. Beyond the fact that everyone benefits, it's also fun! And like the strength we gain in a gym, the more we train our brains, the better we get as a society because we become more high functioning.

We played a lot of games designed to stimulate different types of thinking. I started silently thanking my mom for each day she'd played games with me when I was a kid. I'd always been pretty smart compared to my peers, and it suddenly made sense why I'd been so much further ahead of the other kids when I was young.

I realized some cool facts of life in rehab too. People need to play more—it keeps us young.

People need to read more. It encourages a sense of wonder and stimulates imagination.

People need to talk more and be challenged by the things they're talking about. It creates more intriguing individuals.

People need to laugh more. Even pretending at happiness can create the real thing. I remember in the early days after my accident noticing that people don't smile much these days. At least in L.A., people have a constant look of being preoccupied with whatever they're on their way to do. They seem to forget to enjoy the "now." As I recovered and remembered that, I endeavored never to go back to that state of mind myself.

I was extremely happy that things were getting better for me. I could see my life improving week by week.

The way I've described rehab to people is like the Wizard of Oz. You know the moment in the movie when the black-and-white film changes to color? Do you remember that feeling you had when that happened? That was like my life. I could see and feel the wonder of the color repainting my life, and it was awesome!

Twenty-One

~

"Against the Wind"

There were still mental issues going on, like the inability to sleep on a regular basis. I'd wake up four or five times a night, and I'd started falling asleep without warning, like a narcoleptic.

My temper was also still short, but as my brain regenerated connections to previously inaccessible areas, the frustrations with my inabilities began to diminish as new pathways to them were re-created.

Some areas of my brain responded quickly and others didn't.

My memory was still an issue, and I still had panic attacks because of my inability to recall certain visuals or bits of information. My ability to be confused by others, especially if they were being vague, was still there, and my ability to reason with people through disagreements was still low. I also dealt with aphasia a lot, and though I haven't talked about it much by name, I have in reference. As a clinical term, aphasia refers to the inability to comprehend or produce language—spoken, written, or read. Do you remember those examples I gave about listening to people but not understanding a word they were saying? That's aphasia.

Another example of aphasia that was a regular nuisance was not knowing certain basic words. For instance, I remember agonizing over those things on my shirt that fastened one side to the other. What on earth were they? I've mentioned how I couldn't comprehend anything I read, but I could still type sixty-five words a minute. I could type it but not read it with any sense of understanding. That's aphasia. Aphasia has a lot of other symptoms too, but some of the ones I experienced, for instance, were not being able to remember the names of basic objects, like my example of the buttons. I also experienced a type of aphasia called "dysprosody," although this didn't happen to me very often.

The way I understand dysprosody is that it's an alteration in a person's ability to match an appropriate inflection to a specific type of speech.

For instance, I'd sometimes create awkward situations for myself by using inflections on words that completely changed the message I was trying to send. It became very hard to make a certain point about something based on the wrong inflection. I'll give you an example.

I was riding with a female friend, a sort of feminist type, in her car, and I noticed a woman in traffic who'd almost caused an accident. I wasn't sure if she'd seen it, but I wanted to point out the woman so my friend could stay away from her and keep us safe. I only wanted to offer an observation, but it came out very differently and created a completely charged situation. Here's what I wanted to say:

"Watch out, that woman isn't driving too well."

Here's how it came out:

"Watch out, that WOMAN isn't driving too well."

Another aspect of aphasia I suffered from often was when I couldn't enunciate my words very well. There were times when I'd be talking, and I'd miss consonants or vowel sounds altogether, so my speech sounded almost drunk. This didn't happen all the time, and I'd be hard-pressed to say exactly when it happened most, but in my memory, it seemed that when I'd get excited to share something in conversation, it was like my mouth couldn't keep up with my mind's ability to think it. I'd start stringing half-formed words together and run through an almost unintelligible sentence. Oddly enough, nobody ever commented on this, but I was always aware that I'd done it. I guess they were trying to be nice. Whatever the reason, I was thankful.

The bottom line on the whole rehab experience was that even with the things I was still struggling with, a lot of my life seemed to be getting better. As I worked on the various parts of my brain, the stronger they'd become. The stronger they'd become, the better grasp I'd start to get on the information formulated or processed there. As that happened, my functioning became higher as well. I was marching uphill, and it felt good to be getting closer to the top of the mountain.

*D*URING THAT FIRST TRIP ON ROUTE 66, *we were driving through Missouri when my dad explained that he'd been just my age the first time he'd driven on Route 66 with his parents. First time? I didn't know he'd been on it at all before. My grandparents hadn't given me any clue that they'd been on it before either.*

Still, it was an uncommon treat to hear anything about my dad's past. Intrigued about my father, as any boy is, I wanted to learn anything I could about our family's history.

He shared how my grandparents had planned a family vacation for everyone to see the World's Fair and to visit relatives in California. My dad and Uncle Larry had packed their bags for the trip, hopped in the car, and expected to have a fun family vacation on Route 66 on their way to the West Coast. The break from the extreme rigors of farm work must have felt like a luxury almost too good to believe.

As it turned out, it wasn't to be believed. Once they were several states from home, my grandparents told them that neither of the boys would be going home. Huh?

No, there'd be no return to their life back on the farm. The life they'd just left, they'd left for good.

My grandparents had already arranged that they'd finish up high school in a new town: Midland, Michigan, a hundred miles or more away. They wouldn't be allowed to say good-bye to their friends, to any of the animals they'd cared for over the past several years, and there'd be no graduation from the school they'd attended their whole lives. They'd just be gone. In the fall, they'd be new students in a new place with a new life and no friends.

Remember, this was in the day before cell phones and the Internet. They had no way of letting anyone know what had happened to them. If you didn't have someone's address, you had no way of writing them a letter, and as a teenager, how many of your friends' home addresses do you think the average farm boy has? Your neighbors weren't right next door either, because you had a farm surrounding you, and even seeing other addresses wasn't so common. Phones weren't the common household items teenagers use today, and if you had any phone numbers to call, you didn't have many, and you might need permission to call in the first place.

My dad and Uncle Larry had basically been tricked out of their home state and then ambushed with the news when they were so many states away that jumping out of the car wouldn't be practical.

It seemed a cruel thing to do, and it was my dad's first experience on Route 66. "Get your kicks," eh?

  I'd known that my dad's life on the farm ended around the time he was in tenth grade, but what I never knew were the circumstances of that move. I was a little shell-shocked. My dad's family wasn't big on sharing dirty laundry, and what was private between them as people wasn't expected to be shared with anyone outside that circle.

  So, when my dad started talking about his first Route 66 trip, I had no idea that he'd drop such a bombshell on what had gotten him off the farm all those years before. The impetus behind it had been that my grandpa had gotten a new job and had found someone else to run the family farm. Therefore, the move to Midland for everyone had become possible. Just like that, the farming days were done.

  The story spun my head so wildly because I couldn't even conceive of my grandparents doing something like this to their sons. I mean, picture yourself in the same situation. You pack a bag thinking you're going on vacation and unbeknownst to you, you just moved.

  What?

  The kicker is that no one even knew where my dad had disappeared to. He was just gone. Any relationships he had were inconsequential to my grandparents when they made the decision, and he was helpless to do anything about it. My dad and uncle were being herded to a new place much like cattle. Only, I didn't think of either of them as cattle, and I was stymied as to how my grandparents could treat them that way.

  I knew exactly the bitterness and the feeling of having a hole in your chest something like that can cause because of what had happened with Grandpa Goss being removed from my life. If I'd known that the last time I saw Grandpa Goss was truly going to be the last time for a while, I'd have latched on to him and never let go. He'd been ripped from my life, causing a huge amount of damage. An experience like that creates a subliminal question in a kid's mind: "Who wants to get close to people if the people you love most are going to be ripped away without a vote from you?" It created an extreme element of distrust and fear in me, and suddenly, my dad's sometime irreverent attitude toward his parents made sense.

  In fairness, I'd gotten a break. It took a few years, but Grandpa Goss and I did reconnect. When I saw him again for the first time at Uncle Mark's wedding, I was in third grade. He called out to me excitedly from a pew in the back of the church, but I'd been away from him for about three years, and my little eight-year-old brain didn't compute. Without even a picture of him during those years, his face had simply vanished from my memory.

  He had his arms outstretched to me and was sitting beside his new wife. I had no idea who he was or who she was and didn't budge until someone said, "It's okay ... go say 'hi' to Grandpa Goss."

When my mind made the connection, I was wrapped around his neck faster than lightning to a rod. I loved my grandpa tremendously, and in the years since, I'd been sad, hurt, and angry that people had made that decision to take him from me because of their own quarrels.

Unfortunately, I was never able to fully open myself up to him again over the years. Because I couldn't bear the pain of ever losing him again, something in my head simply wouldn't let me. It was there in my heart, but I just couldn't access or express it. A few years later, when he got cancer, I'm embarrassed to say I struggled to even visit him in the hospital.

When he passed away a short time after, I lost any opportunity with him forever. From that point on, I remained bitter toward the people who'd caused my inability to re-embrace the security of a grandpa who'd loved me like a son and had never shown me anything but goodness. I still ache with regret that he often asked why I didn't come see him more often in the hospital, but I simply couldn't face losing him again. But at least in reconnecting with him, things were made right in that way. He knew I loved him, and I was sure of that. I was also extremely happy for it.

The circumstances were different when my dad's life was derailed, but I thought the dynamics were just about the same. Sure, he hadn't always enjoyed being a workhorse, but he'd made a life of it, probably had a few lifelong friends, and he didn't deserve to be made a farmer to simply have the farm life ripped away from him. His entire identity had been made only to be wiped away by his own parents! Like my family, they had probably thought they were looking out for him and the family.

I instantly understood his sometimes skeptical distrust of my Grandpa and Grandma Rice. I'd grown to feel the same way about the judgment of the people in my mom's family who'd been "looking out for me" when they decided to break all our connections to my grandpa. After a senseless loss, you realize you'd like more say in your own life than what other people may be willing to give you. You want to find some good in it, but how can you?

Suddenly, I didn't see my grandparents as the innocents or celebrities I'd always believed them to be in the tensions I always felt simmering between them and my dad. In truth, they'd caused it. They'd set it up, and when it came back to bite them through his attitude or behavior, they acted like victims who enjoyed the sympathetic attitude of their grandson. What they should have been doing was apologizing to my dad for how indifferently they'd considered him and my uncle back then. Only they never did.

But it was my dad's life, not mine, and he'd obviously made good of it. Had he not been uprooted from the life he knew, he wouldn't have been in such a hurry to escape it on his own terms. Maybe he wouldn't have stopped in Flint, Michigan, to "make a few bucks," at Buick before heading out with a pocket full of money and his true goal of living and surfing in California. But Dad never made it out to California. In fact, he never made it out of Flint because he met my mom, and from there, the rest was history for me. But the story stuck in my head and made me wish I could have made it right for my dad, the way reconnecting with Grandpa Goss had made it right for me.

Twenty-Two

~

"Rolling Down the Hills"

IN TAMMY'S OFFICE, she had a picture of Half Dome, a mountain peak in Yosemite National Park. I'd told her what an allegory I thought it was and that I hoped to make it to the top of my own figurative Half Dome with her help. Beyond that, I made it a goal to climb to the literal top of Half Dome upon graduation from rehab. A sort of symbolic journey of all I'd managed to endure while going through my MTBI climb out of hell.

I made the actual climb a year later. It was arduous, exhausting, and it left me with blisters on my feet that actually seemed analogous to the figurative journey I'd taken to the top of the mental mountain with Tammy. The other similarity was that as I stood at the top of that gallant granite peak, an unexpected storm came up that necessitated a hasty departure back down.

Just as we got off the peak, right when we should have been celebrating our victory, a huge bolt of lightning burst from the sky, exploding a tree just fifty yards to our left and creating an incinerating fire that began to devour it. As the thunder crackled in our ears and the sky opened up in a torrent, we recognized that a huge storm had arrived and we needed to do what we could to avoid getting fried by the next angry bolt. There was a danger of being struck by lightning if I stayed up there too long, and as I came down from the top of the rock, my friends and I actually did feel some static electricity jolts through the cables we held to steady our descent. Very scary.

A seeming victory followed by an unexpected, angry storm. The same thing was just around the corner in my family. It would be my darkest hour. Before that, though, I'd get a view from my own figurative mountaintop.

Thanksgiving was coming up. It felt good to know I'd be going home to my family with the good news that I was recovering and in a good place with carrying on with my life. I felt truly at peace.

What I didn't know was how short-lived that peace would be or how the trip home was going to affect me. That storm I alluded to earlier? It was upon me.

Maybe I was getting too used to the familiarity of a routine again, or perhaps I wasn't prepared for the randomness of visiting unfamiliar spots after such a long a while ... I don't know. Whatever it was, I have no explanation for what happened next, but I felt shaky almost from the moment my plane took off for Michigan.

Even though I'd technically arrived back on home turf, I hadn't lived in Michigan in well over a decade, so in the midst of my recovery, I was a little on edge being away from my familiar routine in Los Angeles. My day-to-day ritual of going back and forth to the now normal structure and expectations of rehab had given me a great deal of stability. It wasn't until I left it behind that I came to realize just how important it had become.

I questioned from my anxiety how much recovering I'd actually done. I was on familiar ground again but without any structure or routine, I was right back to reacting out of my amygdala, and it didn't feel good. Was it possible that all the progress I'd made wasn't really from me at all but from the comfort of the structure rehab had provided?

I'd only be back home for week, but now I realized that amount of time was long enough to feel apprehensive about. I'd not had any panic attacks around my family before, but I was getting that familiar jumpiness that always accompanied them.

No one in my family had seen me in that state, and I didn't want them to now. I was supposed to be getting better. Claiming I was getting better and freaking out at two in the morning would be a contradiction of my now increasingly stable norm, but for them, it may just indicate that "better" was enough to seriously worry about. I was stressed about it. I didn't want anyone to be concerned.

It wasn't like I thought I should talk about it, either. My dad is the kind of guy who generally tries to focus on the positive, sometimes to the detriment of any negative stuff that may actually be happening, so I already knew he wouldn't want to hear anything that might upset that apple cart. That would include anything about the extent of my damage, the rehab experience, or the things I'd been dealing with on a regular basis since my accident. All that my dad would want to know was that his son was okay, and if I'd go along with his desire, I felt things would go a lot smoother than if I started unloading about things I had no answers for. My dad has a tendency to get uncomfortable or upset by things he is unfamiliar with, and I didn't want to be the cause of that discomfort. I chose to play it safe with him and let him see what he wanted to see, which was that I was all right. Just not at the time, because I really felt like I could lose it at any moment.

In fact, I felt about as unstable as I'd felt in several months, maybe even since starting my rehab.

I was feeling self-conscious too. My family tends to have a high sense of empathetic prowess, so they know when something's off with any one of us. If they knew it now, they didn't say anything, and the fact that they didn't say anything tells me that they didn't know, because they're not shy with their words or concerns.

I probably could have shared my current insecurities and fears with my mom. She's way more of an "accept you as you are" person, but her lack of understanding of what I was experiencing would be enough to cause her some severe anxiety in her own right, and I didn't want that. No, it'd be best to keep a lid on how I was feeling, and maybe it would pass.

It didn't. I was jumpy pretty much 24/7 and I felt my pulse racing even when I was trying to convey that I was cool and collected. I started to understand the old saying "I need a vacation from my vacation." Instead of needing a vacation from all the fun and activity I'd had on a regular vacation, though, I needed a break from the uncertain timelines, schedules, and unknown expectations of where I'd be and who I'd be with. I was tired and anxious, and of course, that affected my ability to sleep.

Not that I shared that with anyone. Oddly enough, I wasn't having any of the narcoleptic episodes I'd had in California, so while I knew I needed sleep, I figured not sleeping would at least prevent me from waking up in the midst of a panic attack. And since clearly a week without sleep wouldn't be possible, maybe I could look at the prospect of simply minimizing my sleep. Very stupid of me, I know.

Antianxiety medications had worked best for me, like those prescribed by Dr. Ludwig. Although they didn't keep every bit of anxiety out of my life, they sure helped with about 90 percent of it. In fact, it wasn't until my trip back to Michigan that I realized they weren't 100 percent effective. Now that I was there, however, I knew different. The dosage I was taking definitely wasn't covering the level of anxiety I was experiencing.

At my mom's, not sleeping was an easy thing to explain away. I was one of those old-fashioned folks who didn't have cable on my TV at home, so while I was at her place, with every movie channel ever imagined plus some, I was able to rationalize being awake at four a.m. by saying that I'd gotten interested in whatever movie was on her movie channel. My mom is a huge movie buff, so she'd totally understand that rationale.

At my dad's place, things were different. Dad had been raised on a farm, where it was early to bed, early to rise, "keeps a man healthy, wealthy, and wise." He's not really into TV or movies either, so the guy turns in almost as soon as the sun sets. I mean, it's dark out! What else are you supposed to do? Staying awake with nothing to occupy my time would not be a simple feat.

I hoped to become so completely exhausted that when my body actually did force me to sleep, I'd stay there instead of waking up in the midst of screaming bloody murder. The big drawback was that in the morning, when my dad and stepmom woke up and believed I'd been asleep as long as they had been, they'd naturally wake me up to get my day started, and no matter what small amount of sleep I'd had, I'd be expected to take part in the day's activities with as much energy as everyone else, which would basically be impossible. Throw in the three-hour time difference between Michigan and the West Coast, and my sleep schedule would be massacred anyway. However I look at it, I was in way over my head.

I was becoming irritable to the tenth power.

I was going to be spending Thanksgiving with my mom's family, where I knew there'd be less scrutiny on my behavior and enough laughter to keep my anxiety levels as low as possible. Well, somehow that morning, my mom made the comment that she needed to stop and get gas on the way to where my aunts, uncles, and cousins would be gathering.

When she took a little too long in getting ready, we ended up leaving for Thanksgiving dinner almost an hour later than planned. Normally, I'd have just rolled with this, but this time, for whatever reason, I was in no condition to endure any deviations from the structure of our established plans. I was as edgy and grouchy as I had been in a long, long time, so I started getting fidgety.

Since I could tell I was quickly getting out of line, I employed the tried-and-true practice of avoiding conflict that I used back in California. When I started feeling my temper rising, I'd instantly go to my car or to my room or anywhere away from the source of what or who was upsetting me. Doing this had kept people from witnessing my "wig-outs" and had probably been best for all involved. The part of that plan involving the escape to my room would still work pretty well at my mom's house because her extra room is upstairs, and that was where I was sleeping, far away from anyone else.

By the time she was ready to go, she felt bad that she'd made us late, and being as sensitive as she is, she apologized for taking so long. For whatever reason, I couldn't get the anger to subside. It was still welling up, and I was having a hard time controlling it. When I came downstairs and she said she was sorry, I chose to head straight out the door and to the car without saying a word. I couldn't risk saying anything. I just needed to get out of there.

I grabbed a snow shovel and decided to channel my aggression on the sidewalk. No one had shoveled it off yet, so why not me?

Unfortunately, this only irritated me more. My mom and Doug had been a couple almost from the moment they met in 1989. In all the years they've been together, he's been extremely good to her, but for some reason, on this day, the fact that he hadn't shoveled the sidewalk for her to walk out to her car safely really got under my skin. I wondered, since he'd decided not to go, whether he'd intended for her to shovel the sidewalk while he stayed inside nice and cozy. I felt my anger rising. Of course, the fact that she put up with it only upset me more. I thought she was being weak by not taking a stand against him. Forget that she probably didn't know there was a stand to take. In my twisted head, it made sense to me, and that was all that mattered at that moment.

She came out, finally prepared to go, and got into the driver's seat of her car. I put the shovel away and was simmering along, trying to think of whatever I could to distract myself and get settled. Even with my ever-growing faulty logic, I was still aware that it was about me being in a bad place, but it was useless. I might as well have been a roaring lion waiting to devour whatever came my way. I could feel myself getting crazy.

Either way, my poor mom had no way of avoiding my anger, and it didn't take long to show itself. When I noticed we were heading the wrong way from the direction we were supposed to be going, I didn't say anything at first, but I couldn't hold that stance very long. We were already late. Why were we going farther away from our destination?

I asked her, and she said she'd changed her mind and wanted to go to a different gas station than the one that was on the way. There was another one not too far out of the way where the gas was always two to three cents cheaper. You're talking to the guy who will drive ten minutes out of the way to save a penny, so this should have made sense and gotten support from me.

Not today though. I flew into a rage and demanded that we turn around. We were going fifteen minutes out of our way to save two cents a gallon? I angrily yelled that we were already late and asserted that I'd pay the extra two cents, just turn this car around and get going in the right direction.
My mom made the bad decision of sticking to her guns and saying that no, this would be better, higher-quality gas anyway.

In protest, I threw open the car door and jumped out of the car.

My mom stopped in the middle of the road, the passenger door still open and nearly ripped off from the momentum of the car stopping so quickly.

I started marching up the street, and due to the line of cars building up behind her, my mom was forced to move on down the road without me. I know being put in this position must have devastated her, but I wasn't in my right mind, and although I knew that what I was doing was wrong, I simply felt unable to do anything differently.

She circled around and came back up the road toward me. She was very calm, but I could hear the hurt in her voice when she called out for me to get back in the car.

I wasn't having it. My brain was going to do what it was going to do. I kept marching up the road. Even though I knew I was out of line, I couldn't stop myself.

Soon enough, she'd turned around again and came up the road beside me. She called again for me to please get in the car. This time I listened and got back in.

I don't remember what we talked about. I'm sure we did talk, though, because my mom is the kind of person who wants to make things right. I'm sure she would have naturally assumed that she'd done something wrong instead of it being entirely me who was out of line. We somehow ended up at Thanksgiving dinner.

I have very little memory of the rest of that day. I don't know if I've repressed it or whether I was just exhausted by it all, but beyond acting like an idiot to my mom, I don't recall any real interaction between me and my family at all that year. It's as if it just slipped away from me. I do know that I decided sleep would be a good thing again, regardless of the danger of panic attacks. I'd hurt my mom enough, and I hoped that ample rest might prevent it from happening any more than it already had.

My mom is very forgiving, though. She knew I was in rehab, so she talked a lot about things from my past, trying to reconnect me to memories I might have had or places I may have been. Maybe if I could make some connection to those old familiar things, I could make breakthroughs in reconnecting the parts of my brain that weren't providing necessary info when I needed it.

My dad was very much like this too.

While I was at his house, he took me out to his garage, where I saw a ton of things from over the years, things that broke through that mental concrete to make some reconnections. Mostly, because my dad tends to be very mild-mannered, just being in a calm, safe environment with him opened me up to relaxing and taking it all in again.

I saw a box of toys I'd had as a kid stacked away at the top of his garage.

I remembered those! I liked those!

It sounds so simple, but I really started feeling connected to whom I'd been before my accident, and suddenly, that guy didn't seem so far away.

However, I left Michigan feeling very ashamed of how I'd treated my mom that day.

Twenty-Three

~

CHRISTMAS WAS RIGHT AROUND THE CORNER, and I'd made plans to return home again just a few short weeks later. However, there was one source of aggravation on this trip that kept needling at me: that unshoveled sidewalk at my mom's house.

A month earlier, I'd shoveled that thing at least two or three times, and during this trip, I found myself doing it three or four more times. Generally, right before we were getting ready to go somewhere.

One morning, I came down the stairs and asked Doug where my mom was.

"Outside," he replied from his seat at the table in the kitchen.

Outside? What the heck could she be doing out there? It was Michigan in winter and it was cold out. My mom was nearly fifty-four years old at the time, and it didn't seem like the best place for her to be just "hanging out." Ultimately, I came to know what this meant. Hearing she was "outside" was really code for "out shoveling the sidewalk."

This upset me because Doug was perfectly capable of doing such a task. The fact that my mom was outside shoveling snow when a good man was sitting inside enjoying the TV and heated home made absolutely no sense to me.

Initially, I'd been shoveling the sidewalk because I didn't want my mom to hit a spot of ice and fall on her way to the car. I'd told her this and also expressed my frustration with Doug for not doing this for her. She wasn't just fifty-four, she was overweight and fifty-four. If you know anything about areas with extreme winter climates, you know that more people suffer heart attacks shoveling sidewalks in winter than doing anything else—it happens a lot.

I didn't want to see my mom out there shoveling a sidewalk, slipping on some ice, and ending up having a heart attack from overexerting herself. I'd told my mom this. I didn't want her shoveling the sidewalk. This was Doug's job, and the fact that I was the one shoveling their sidewalk made no sense to me.

It's probably no surprise after my road rage the previous month that my mom didn't want me getting upset by Doug's lack of effort. Therefore, she'd wait until I jumped in the shower to get ready in the morning, and then she'd run outside and shovel the sidewalk so I'd be none the wiser.

The only problem is that I don't take very long to get ready in the morning, so I was out and ready before she was done with the shoveling.

I sat on that frustration during both my Thanksgiving and Christmas trips home. Why was Doug allowing my mom to shovel the sidewalk? Keep in mind, I wasn't dealing with frustration like a normal person anyway, but add in something that is justifiable to get upset about, and you've got a powder keg situation waiting to happen.

Before my accident, I'd have calmly talked to Doug about it, but I was still having such a hard time monitoring and controlling my emotions that I chose not to talk to him for fear of things getting out of control. I'd told my mom I wanted her to talk to Doug about it and remind him he should be taking care of household duties like that so that not only she wouldn't have to do it, I wouldn't have to either.

Doug is no small man, maybe 6'1" or 6'2" and well over two hundred pounds. Shoveling a short sidewalk isn't a big job for a man of his height or stature. My mom is maybe 5'6" and not the strongest gal in the world. It ate at me.

And ate at me.

Three hours before I left Michigan, I noticed the shoveling hadn't been done and loudly proclaimed we'd be leaving in just a few hours and would need to get that thing shoveled beforehand. Doug was present for this announcement, and my mom agreed it needed to be done.

That's why when I came down the stairs that final time a few hours later with my suitcase in hand and ready to go to the airport, I was shocked to see my mom outside shoveling the sidewalk yet again.

I went bounding out the door.

"Mom, what are you doing?"

"I'm shoveling the sidewalk."

Yes, I could see that. I swiped the shovel from her, admonished her, and asked if she'd talked to Doug about this.

Not yet.

That's all I needed to hear. I told her she needed to talk to him, or else when I was finished, I was going to talk with him about it, something I really didn't want to have to do. She disappeared inside the house and, a few minutes later, just as I was finishing, she came back out.

"Did you talk with him?"

She told me she'd do it later.

As my mom grabbed the scraper to clean off the car's windshield, I went back into the house. There was Doug still sitting in his bathrobe and watching TV.

I told him "Happy New Year" and that I wanted to say good-bye. I also asked if I could request a favor of him. In fifteen years, I'd never asked him for anything, so I didn't think this was hugely inappropriate. Anyhow, he said yes, I could ask.

"Doug, my mom's got a lot of extra weight on her these days and she's fifty-four years old. Can you do me a favor and instead of letting her shovel the sidewalk this winter, will you do it instead?" Phew. I'd gotten it out calmly. Successfully.

He got up from his chair thoughtfully and wished me a "Happy New Year" while following me to the door. I turned around once outside on the porch, expecting him to meet me at the door and give me the simple "yes" I was hoping for.

Instead, he slammed the door on me.

I was incensed. You'd have thought I asked for nuclear secrets or something. In a million years, I'd have never guessed asking him to look out for my mom a little better would get the door slammed in my face.

I opened the door back up and asked him what he was doing. I'd made a simple request. He tried to push the door shut on me again.

I shoved my foot in and kept the door from closing. He told me I'd been an invited guest to the house and could also be easily uninvited. The thought that he'd arrogantly uninvite me from my mother's house, whether he lived there or not, was enough to multiply my anger. I'd done relatively well up to this point, but with no emotional governor, my temper left the atmosphere. As he was about to find out, once I'd lost it, there was no coming back.

He'd had his finger through the crack in the door pointing in my face. Big mistake. I slapped it away with one hand and shoved him backward with the other. He tried to recover, but I was through the door and on him. Every move he tried to make, I anticipated and beat, ready to oblige anything he brought on. He was going to respect my wishes for my mom's care whether he wanted to or not, and I let him know what would happen to him if he didn't. I had a hold of him by the collar or throat, I don't remember which, when I threatened, "If she has a heart attack out there, I will put your ass in the ground!"

I was out of control, but I was very aware of how dangerous my temper was. As I saw him muster some anger of his own, I issued a warning.

"Don't think you're gonna get mean, 'cuz I promise I'm way meaner."

He tried to push past me, but I shoved him with enough force that he lifted awkwardly off his feet. I refused to let him dismiss what I was saying. He'd gotten me to this angry point, and I was going to make sure it wasn't in vain. He was going to stay right here until he heard me and took me seriously. The only problem was he was just sort of smiling at me now in a taunting manner, and the more he smiled, the more pissed and determined I was to drive my point home. I threw him all over the kitchen like a puppet, and he lost his smile fairly quickly.

My mom came running in at that point, already in tears, begging me to stop throwing him around. I remember her getting in between us and telling me to get out of the house. This only upset me more, and I refused to leave.

After my parents' divorce, I'd seen my mom get treated badly by men she'd dated while I was a child. I made a vow to myself that as an adult, I'd never let that happen. That was a decision made with the rational mind of a man who didn't like violence. Now here I was with anything but a rational mind, and I was determined to stick to that vow, violence or not. I was fixated on making sure that Doug heard me today.

The problem was that I saw fear in my mom's eyes, and it took all the fire out of me. I felt so ashamed, even in the midst of my behavior. I knew my actions were wrong, even if my intentions were good.

Instead of the usual love in her eyes, there was terror. Her look silently pleaded, "Why are you doing this to us?"

I had no answers. What I'd wanted to do was help my mom, and what I'd done was hurt her more than I could have imagined. Beyond hurting her, I'd hurt Doug, who up to this point had never been anything but kind to me. To go from zero to 100 and treat him so lowly was a rotten thing, but again, I couldn't stop myself. All I could do was watch my actions and hang on until I was finished.

My mom begged me to let go of him, and eventually I relented, but I still angrily demanded an agreement that he'd shovel the sidewalk from here on out. Instead, with a nervously shaking hand, he reached out for a coffee mug on the table to maybe take a drink and steady himself.

I grabbed his hand, forcing the mug back to the table. I felt evil … in total control of him, and even in the midst of it, it was scary to be this way. However, something in my head said no matter what I had to do, I was going to break this man, the same man who for fifteen years, regardless of the sidewalk, had been nothing but good to my mother.

I'd stripped his dignity and humiliated him. All over an unshoveled sidewalk.

I was insane. I knew it at the time, but I didn't know how to find my way out of it.

Mom stayed in there between us, crying and begging me to leave him alone. She told me the sidewalk didn't matter. She said anything she could to get me to snap out of it. I guess it worked because at some point, and I don't remember when, I gave up and left the house. I was still furious, but at least Doug was in one piece.

I raged on as Mom drove me to the airport. I chastised her for siding against her own blood when she was being defended. My logic was gone though. She had probably just prevented me from killing him, and I'm ashamed to say that, except that brain damage will make you do dangerous things you never conceived of prior to the injury.

I made it to the plane completely exhausted. I don't really remember getting there, because, again, anger took so much out of me that everything became foggy. My mind raced with the speed of a cyclone during these episodes, but afterward, I'd crash into a haze before falling asleep to recover.

I couldn't explain why I'd humiliated him in the extreme manner I had. It could have just as easily been a discussion, or at worst, a verbal argument. Instead, I'd pushed it to a physical confrontation, and I'd have to deal with the fallout. I also knew I had no recourse for explaining my behavior because I'd mostly hidden the extent of my brain damage, so this would seem like a choice I'd made from my own rational mind, although I was anything but rational.

I learned later that Doug had been so shaken up that he'd nearly left my mom that day. He'd been ready to go by the time she got back from the airport. After all those years together, I'd done something that could have irreparably damaged a relationship that had nothing to do with me but everything to do with my mom's happiness. Doug was her best friend and had doted on her for years, cooking her dinner every night, and generally just adoring her company. He'd made the mistake of not shoveling a sidewalk, and for that, he was no longer safe in their house, and he felt he needed to get away.

I'm not sure what it was that kept him there, but it was probably his love for my mom. I'm just glad he stayed. Through my recovery in rehab, I eventually got to a point where I could show my face again. I worked up the nerve to apologize to him for my behavior. I was surprised he'd even talk to me at all, and I'm sure he'd have never brought it up. When I told him I was sorry, he only said, "It's okay. We both messed up that day."

He'd never called the police on me or did anything that would have hurt me, and why? Because he had the wherewithal to not want to hurt my mom. Unlike me.

I felt like a heel, but they both seemed to forgive me. To be honest, I'm not sure that I've fully forgiven myself yet. But that's my family. They are loving and supportive to the end.

*B*ACK IN 1985, *my dad and I were headed for New Mexico and had a good time driving across the country together. I'd wait until he nodded off, and then I'd run the speedometer up to about ninety, feeling like I'd finally been unleashed on the world.*

I remember him waking up in Amarillo, Texas, and figuring out that with the miles we'd traveled from Michigan, we'd mysteriously averaged fifty-six miles per hour in a day when the federal speed limit was fifty. Oops. I was busted.

Noting the point was all the correction he gave me, though, and I noticed that somewhere in there, he was quietly amused by my newly adopted "born to be wild" attitude.

Somewhere along the trip, we'd stopped at a shop on Route 66 and stumbled on a really cool black-and-white photo that had been framed and placed just inside the front entrance of a gas station. It said that it'd once been on the cover of Life magazine. On the left-hand side of the photo was an old Texaco station, and on the right-hand side, an old auto repair shop that said "West End Garage." The sky was filled with billowy white clouds and going right up through the middle of the photo between the buildings and toward the horizon was an endless road. The caption below the photo simply said, "Somewhere in Arizona on Route 66 – 1947." It was a breathtaking snapshot in time.

Now standing on Route 66 in 1985, my dad and I looked at it for a long moment before he said, "Wouldn't it be neat to find that exact spot today and see what it looks like?"

Are you kidding? I'd just gotten my driver's permit and set a land speed record coming across the USA. You didn't have to twist my arm to get me behind the wheel to go find that spot.

We headed on down the road. For a lot of the way along Route 66, I was captivated. I discovered that the railroad tracks and the trains I'd always loved—and that were quickly disappearing in various parts of the country—ran parallel to the road for a lot of the way west. Trains! Suddenly I wasn't just heading across our country, I was in a time warp and connecting back to a time in my life that still felt pure and unblemished. This Route 66 was somehow magically transcendent and amazing for being so.

We made it to New Mexico and saw my grandparents on that trip, but before the whole thing was over, we'd gotten back on the road and fol-

lowed Route 66 all the way to Flagstaff, Arizona. We didn't find the Life magazine picture spot, but I filed it in my brain as something I'd like to do, and thought if I ever got the chance, I'd find the spot for my dad and let him know where it was and what I found.

In the meantime, I just needed to get through being a teenager. Life felt like it had just begun at 90 mph around Tulsa....

Twenty-Four

~

"One Belief Away"

AMAZINGLY, THERE WAS NO ANGER MANAGEMENT group at my rehab. You'd think that would be the first service provided to a group like us, but there was nothing. That seemed like the most blatant oversight you could ever make when it came to dealing with people who had suffered a TBI. Instead, we talked about anger management issues in therapy, but fairly briefly.

As I progressed further in treatment, I was reconnecting my abilities to think rationally through situations in ways that took away some of the anger management issues. That hadn't been possible earlier in my program. The more I worked, however, the easier it was becoming. That's not to say my anger problems immediately vanished, they just became less and less frequent.

As my brain regained abilities to do certain things, more normality was restored. It was as if a missing piece of the puzzle was found and added to re-create a fuller picture of how it should be functioning within itself. My emotional governors started to fall back into place, and my normal processing started to kick into gear again. Once my brain learned how to do these things correctly, it would follow its own directions of how to do it again next time.

Then I noticed something really amazing. With all of the new roadways created in my brain through rehabilitation, in some cases, a lot of my thoughts, emotions, and abilities began functioning far better than they had prior to my accident. My thinking was sharp, almost crystal clear. My short- and long-term memories seemed to be working as well as they had in fifteen years. My processing was markedly improved. It was as if I'd gone to a boot camp for my mind. The road was smooth and the engine seemed to be firing on all cylinders.

This being said, it didn't mean my knowledge of everything lost actually returned. I lost all sports knowledge due to my accident, and once it was gone, it was gone. Kind of like those stretches of Route 66 that have been swallowed back up by the desert or cut off by the new interstate. My brain became like one of the little towns that were abandoned once Route 66 was bypassed in the late '70s and early '80s. It didn't mean the towns weren't there anymore. They are, and you can drive past many today, mere feet from I-40 and still in plain sight of the new road. They're just abandoned and unreachable, with no people living there anymore. Since the old route is no longer serviceable, there's no real way to get to them from the new I-40, even though you're a stone's throw away. Instead, they became ghost towns. That's what happened to some of the info in my brain. It was unreachable and became abandoned.

In the same way that new towns were planned for development and constructed along I-40, any new knowledge of sports for me would have to be planned and reconstructed along fresh "roadways" of my own in rehab. It would take some time, maybe, but at least now it was possible. I'd just have to do it from scratch.

In addition to a quickly healing brain, I also had a quickly rising bill at rehab. With no job, paying for it had been impossible initially, so my old friend and lawyer Tracy Baer went to Mr. Cell-phone's insurance company. Nearly two years later, my rehab was paid for in full with a few dollars to spare. That was a relief.

A few months before I finished my rehab, I also got my first opportunity back in the movie industry to produce a film. It was nothing major, just a short twenty-minute independent film to have fun learning on. That's what we did too—we had fun. I also realized that although things hadn't ended so well at my old job, I had learned enough in my time there to produce a film. My boss had done his job of teaching me after all; I just hadn't realized it until now.

Since my recovery was incomplete, my new friend and producing partner, Ian Eyre, had no idea how full his hands were going to be. All he knew was that I'd had a brain injury, and it had put me out of the movie business for a while. What he didn't know was the figurative and literal headaches he'd have to deal with in not only managing to finish the film but also trying to manage me, at times. And this is an interesting point because at the time we did the film, I'd been in rehab for quite a long time and thought I was doing quite well. I assured him I was up to the task.

One night, we'd been driving to a set with a camera in the back of our equipment truck. It so happened that the moon was huge and beautiful that night, and coincidentally, we needed a shot of a moon like that for our film.

Since I was once again enthusiastically exercising the right to use my still valid California driver's license, when he asked to pull into a parking lot so we could set up a camera shot, I did so. The only problem was that because of my still-scattered thinking at the time, once we got into the lot, I started driving in the opposite direction to where we should have been going. I don't remember this, but he tells me that as he continued trying to guide me back to where we could get the "moon shot," I kept circling around the wrong way as if I had no sense at all of what we were trying to do.

On the fifth time around, he got me to the right place to park. There was a straight sprint to a high spot nearby where we'd set up the camera for a great shot. For whatever reason, I started off not toward it but on a zigzagging run all over and generally without a definitive destination. Ian said he became quite frustrated and finally got me to stay with him, but that it was one heck of an ordeal. All told, what should have taken a few moments got stretched into an obstacle course ride and a run through a parking lot and up a hill, resulting in the casualty of one errant shopping cart that got in the way of the truck. Remember: I was making what was considered "good" recovery at this time.

The film with Ian got finished. Was it Citizen Kane? No way. But at least it was a sign of something more I could do. Most important, it was fun.

Producing the film with Ian was a great exercise in experiencing something fun and productive. Even though I wasn't recovered at the time we did it, I felt like I was firing on all cylinders, even if I had "spark knock" from time to time. I'm not sure I'd ever been as good at something in the movie biz as I was at managing a crew of people on a budget and deadlines of time constraints. It was a really great thing for me.

I produced a couple more short films after this, but nothing in the way of the full-length feature films I'd once dreamt of producing. Not only wasn't Hollywood beating down the door of a brain-damaged, ex-acting, out-of-work writer, I wasn't exactly fueled about going out and explaining why I'd been out of it for so long. Just so people could discriminate and ridicule my injury? No. I was looking for something more.

I now had my heart set on doing something bigger. Something that could impact people and bring them happiness.

Twenty-Five

~

"Take It to the Limit"

GRADUATION TIME IS ALWAYS SUCH an exciting time of the year. It was the same way at rehab. There was a funny ritual that included announcements being made over the loudspeaker anytime someone completed their neuro-rehab testing modules, meaning they'd mastered that skill and were ever closer to graduating. I'd completed my modules and had my name announced over the loudspeaker, but on the day Tracy paid my rehab bill from Mr. Cell-phone's insurance money, I was considered done with no graduation. I don't know if they'd been keeping me for the morale boost or what, but it was sad that after all I'd gone through with them, they never officially graduated me. I was just done.

I decided to take a cross-country road trip from the Midwest back to California on whatever parts of the old "Mother Road" I could find. It was symbolic, I thought. Route 66 was actually beginning something of a comeback with tourists, and I was getting to live a comeback of my own. At the beginning of the trip, I went to Michigan and with money left over from the settlement I bought my mom a new car as a "thank you" for all the financial help she'd given me during my recovery. It felt good.

For most of the next year, I traveled as much as I could and finally became a true Route 66 aficionado. Arizona became my favorite Route 66 state, but there are stories all along the old "Mother Road" that made me glad to be alive. It was such a nice, philosophically relaxing break from the real world, but I knew it was too good to last forever. I'd needed a fun year, though, and I was happy to get it. The people were so kind to me, and they had no expectations of who I'd been. They were just happy to make friends with who I was, and I was glad to make friends with them too. I'm happy to say, I made a lot.

Back in California, the folks at the rehab office were laying the foundation for me to get back into the full swing of life. They thought I would be the perfect candidate for working in their marketing department. In that capacity, I'd get to speak for TBI patients, and between my personal experience and my psychology degree, they considered me a shoo-in for such a job. There were no openings as of then, but they assured me that when one opened up, I'd be a natural fit.

Once I came back from traveling "America's Main Street," I decided to really go for some permanence on a street of my own. With the supportive assurance of a marketing job on the horizon, I decided to settle into normalcy, and I bought a house. It was just three miles from the job because I wanted to be close and convenient. While waiting for my job to start, I started a regular habit of going by the rehab center to spread good cheer, keep morale up, and volunteer around the place in whatever ways I could.

Then came the time to actually fill the position. I was immediately blown away to learn that when the staff at the rehab office approached the regional marketing director about me, she wasn't interested at all.

Not interested? At all? How could that be? Everybody in the office treated me like I worked there already, as if hiring me had been a formality. I'd been so convinced of the job, I'd stupidly bought a house. I panicked, but they tried to calm me. They explained that because the marketing director worked out of a different office and didn't know me, she'd been unable to make any mental connection between me and my ability to market the value of TBI rehab.

Hang on a second. The woman had decided that despite my master's in the psych field, my enthusiasm about and experience with recovery, and my belief in rehabilitation, I didn't have the skill set to do marketing in the field of traumatic brain injury? Really? It seemed illogical, but what could I do?

I'd been used to feeling like the star pupil of the place, but now I wasn't so sure of my role. I was the guy the staff looked to as being inspirational in my recovery. In fact, I think they believed in my recovery more than I did. Even now, they reorganized behind me. Privately, I questioned whether I wasn't still seen as damaged goods by the higher-ups. Maybe that's why the marketing director didn't want me.

I'd finished my program, but I wasn't convinced I was better. Maybe that's what the marketing director believed too. I did still feel different from the person I was before my accident. Even though I'd successfully tested out of the areas I'd failed at upon my arrival, and despite the fact that I was now performing at a higher level, any difference at all still left a feeling of being not quite completely better or back to my old self. The fact that people sometimes responded to me differently upon learning of my brain-injured status did nothing to buoy my confidence.

The clinical director in L.A., Prudence, was unruffled by the marketing team's decision. She figured I simply needed to prove my level of dedication to the job and the rehab center, and eventually they would rethink their decision. In the meantime, Prudence asked me if I was willing to volunteer to organize the marketing binders, straighten marketing supplies—anything that would put me in the way of anyone in the marketing department. There was no way the regional marketing director could ignore me then.

The company had several offices across the country, so the marketing team spread themselves between various locations. They came through L.A. regularly, and on one of their first days there, I was interested to see some of the different people the marketing director had chosen to be on her team. A few new people had been chosen as well. I just wasn't one of them. As they introduced themselves to the staffers who worked out of the L.A. office, I appeared to be just another employee, not the volunteer I actually was.

One of the new women was particularly interesting to me. One of the benefits of going through my recovery was that I was still pretty good at accurately reading people's emotional process, regardless of what they were trying to portray to the outside world ... my "infant processing." This new woman was intent on presenting a visage of cool collectedness that couldn't possibly have hidden her truly frazzled nature. It was a fragile façade with a little "bull-in-a-china-shop" vibe just waiting to break free. This is what the marketing director wanted?

As one of the new marketing hires, she didn't know exactly where she fit in the big hierarchy, so I could almost see her jockeying for position as soon as she came in the office. She didn't know anything about me or what my position was; she only knew that I was one of the L.A. staff. Beyond that, I didn't stand out as different because I'd worked in clinical settings before and was comfortable in them. As such, she was working extremely hard to sell me on how genuine she was while also trying to figure out who I was and how quickly she could get the supplies she needed from me for her new marketing binder.

I asked her what she was looking for and led her off to find it. We were having a decent, topical conversation when she started jockeying for position between the two of us. Who was I and how long had I worked for the place? Was this position the only one I filled in marketing or was I also a part of something bigger?

I could see this situation unfolding. If I answered that I was somebody in a position of high stature, she was going to be really nice to me. If I said I was a lowly volunteer, she'd instantly start treating me as an underling. She was persistent in trying to figure it out. Who was I?

I decided to really throw the bait in the water.

"I was a patient here," I told her.

"Oh!" she answered, trying to figure out how she should act toward me now.

While she searched for an answer, I found what she'd been looking for in the supply room. As I held it out to her, she took it gingerly and nodded at me like I was retarded. In a very loud voice, she enunciated a slow "THAAANNNNNKKKK YOOOOUU," like I couldn't understand it any other way.

I'd been brain-damaged, not deafened, I thought. But her reaction to me was interesting. Like her boss, she was clearly uncomfortable with my status as a brain-injured person. I was maybe the first brain-injured person she'd ever actually spoken with, and yet, there she was running off to her marketing meeting to learn how to reach other brain-injured patients. She'd just failed at her first opportunity, and yet she was gainfully employed. There I was, the guy who not only organized but also read all the marketing binders from back to front and front to back, and I probably knew more personally about brain injuries than anyone in the place. And yet, I was jobless.

Frustrated, I went to Prudence. I told her there was no way I'd get hired into their marketing department and felt it was futile to keep putting myself in their path. She decided we needed to take another approach and asked me if I'd be interested in doing a seminar at an upcoming community outreach to other healthcare professionals. I'd have to wait a few months, but the owner of the company would be there. She thought if he saw me, maybe we could bypass this shortsighted marketing director and her staff, and work me right into a job through him.

Wow! Public speaking?

I was positive if I did a speaking engagement in front of the owner of the company, a guy I'd met and had good experiences with, I was a shoo-in for a job there.

The day finally came. As I told the audience of various healthcare professionals my story of recovery, the ups, the downs, and the ultimate comeback, at certain points, I had them laughing. At other points, they were in tears. I relayed the importance of what they did as health professionals and how I could never have made it through without the help of people like them. They were moved, and I have to say, I blew it out of the water. You'd have thought I was a celebrity.

It was almost entertaining when the regional marketing director, the same woman who'd wanted nothing to do with interviewing me, came up to me afterward and told me in front of her boss—the owner, no less—that I should be an inspirational speaker.

How could I respond to that? She'd refused to even interview me.

*I*N 1992, *a few years after Dad and I took that trip along Route 66, after a turn in college and with my teenage years long behind me, I moved to California for graduate school. I'd finished my bachelor's degree in psychology and was going to California to get my master's degree in family therapy. I wanted to prevent that traumatic time in my life when my family imploded from happening in the lives of others. What can I say? I'd become a cliché. I was twenty-two. Anyhow, it'd be my first foray into saving the world, and as interested as I was in saving people from trouble, I was excited for what my new life would become.*

Not that anything was guaranteed, because I'd been derailed from saving the world a couple of years earlier. During that time, Grandma Rice begged me not to enlist in the army during Operation Desert Shield. Since all the men in my family had spent time in the U.S. military, it was like a family tradition. Now that a career with GM seemed unattainable, joining the military seemed like the only other family tradition I could follow. She pleaded with me not to put her through it. She said that she'd gone "through hell" when Grandpa Rice was away during World War II, and when my dad was in the army during the '60s, she was terrified he'd be killed in Vietnam. She cried and cried that she was too old to go through this again and convinced me that since I was already in my junior year of college, to finish.

Although I felt like I was missing out on a once-in-a-lifetime experience and the honor of serving my country, I was finally persuaded by my grandpa to listen to Grandma Rice and to finish what I'd started in college. Somewhat begrudgingly, I stayed in school, even when many of my friends were enlisting, and by the time Desert Storm was over, I was nearly ready to graduate.

Less than two years later, there I was, on my way to California to earn a master's degree. Arizona was right on the path west. It was interesting driving through the country again because I saw and remembered a lot of the same sights I'd seen with my dad back in '85. When I came through Arizona, I slowed down to make sure I didn't miss anything that might be that spot he and I had spied in the photo all those years before. I was disappointed once again that I didn't find the spot.

It wouldn't be hard to get me out there. Being on the road was even more in my blood since getting my license, and everything about it connect-

ed me back to a much simpler time in my life. It was a time of USA map puzzles and travels across the country with my family. A time of watching trains link my small hometown to my Grandpa and Grandma Goss's place in Flint in a day when it was really beautiful. A time when America was great, cars were Chevys and Fords, and all our people were building the highest-quality, greatest products in the world. People had jobs and money, and the American Dream was truly within reach for everyone. It was a time when home was the greatest place I'd ever been or could even remember.

Now here I was as an adult, still having fun on the road and exploring the country. The road trip across America in an American-made car made me feel proud to have grown up among the majesty of it all. While I'd probably become "uncool" for being such a staunch holdout to American cars, I didn't care. I was still supporting those loyal American workers who were now all too few, but who were still doing their best to maintain their spots on the line.

For most of the way along Route 66, I was comforted to rediscover that the rail lines I'd seen in 1985 still ran parallel and were still carrying a lot of trains. Once again, my experience on the road and alongside all the trains instantly transported me to the time I'd had with my family as a child. The trains had been a constant in my life, whether at Grandpa and Grandma Goss's home, or with my mom at the grocery store, or even while racing trains with my dad across the USA. I remembered waving to the man in the caboose and knowing it was possible he'd wave to my family somewhere else down the line. Here I was, all the way across the country from Michigan, and Route 66 and all the trains were again helping me feel close to family back home. It was as if waving to one of these guys beside a road that was tied to so much history was like waving into time itself. If I wanted to wave to Grandpa Goss, who'd been gone for several years now and was standing outside time with God Himself, then these same rails that had been around since long before he'd passed could easily carry the message backward or forward through time.

Twenty-Six

~

"Castles Made of Sand"

Almost immediately after my speech to the healthcare professionals, the owner of the rehab company pulled me aside and told me how he'd appreciated me speaking on behalf of his company. He asked me a little bit about what I'd done in the movie biz and suggested that if there was a way for our circles to intersect, the two of us should talk. I told him I did have an idea, and right then, we set up a time for a few weeks later to talk.

Finally, things were taking a turn for the better. It'd taken a long time to set up, but it had happened … a full year after I'd finished rehab. I tried to contain my excitement, but it wasn't easy. All I could do now was wait a few weeks until the meeting could take place.

When the day came, he, Prudence, and the marketing director were all there. But it was the big guy who wanted to know my ideas.

I told him how to reach the TBI patients directly.

I had lots of ideas about infomercials that would be low cost to produce, yet would reach the target audience of insomniacs like I'd been, people who were up at odd hours of the night, wondering what was wrong with them. I envisioned tapping my old contacts in Hollywood and maybe getting some of the producers, companies, or networks to finance and produce a movie of the week.

He loved it. In fact, he shared that my thoughts dovetailed with some of the ideas he had about future directions for his company—a media division. It was forward thinking and unlike anything they'd done before. He'd do it. He simply need to reallocate some of the marketing budget to this new arm of the company to make it happen.

I could have sworn I saw the regional marketing director cringe when she heard this. That concerned me, but I knew she didn't understand. She'd need a TBI patient's experience and vision to understand what we were talking about, and she didn't have it.

By the end of the meeting, we had a tentative plan for going forward. That's all I needed to hear because I was determined I'd make a difference in ways that would expand our company's abilities to help beyond anything they'd conceived of before. I'd take my message to the people who needed to know. Victims, spouses, friends, family members, dogs, cats … you name it. I could make it happen. We were going to not only change some lives, we were going to reclaim some lives and save lives. Not only had I been through the ordeal of rehab to get my day-to-day life back, I was now going to be a productive working member of society again in a position where I had the passion and experience to make a difference. I felt blessed.

I thought God must have allowed me to go through this brain-injury experience because He knew I'd have the passion to reach people like me … people who'd had no one to speak for them before, people who needed kindness. And who doesn't need that?

I waited a few weeks for the final meeting. When I showed up that morning, however, I got the not-so-great surprise that the regional marketing director had forgotten about it. Forgotten? It was clear that she'd slipped back into being a non-fan. I was in no position to put up a fuss, though. She may not believe in what we wanted to do, but I needed her to believe in it eventually, and to do that, I needed to get started in the first place. Working with her might end up being a chore, but the work itself was the most important thing, and I was determined to do a good job, despite her negativity.

The meeting was rescheduled for a few days later. It actually happened the second time, and although the marketing director seemed openly resentful just having to meet me, she nevertheless told me that I'd have a start date just three short weeks away. She did keep harping on about what she felt was a lack in my "skill set," as if someone as "damaged" as I was must be incapable of doing anything of value for the company—certainly a different tone than the owner had communicated. Regardless, the owner had given the word to hire me, and she told me it was going to happen. My start date was September 1.

But something was nagging at me.

The marketing director was clearly opposed. All her body language and vocal tone told me so. Although I was given a start date, her doubts about my deficient skill set made her opinion clear. She didn't like me. I was getting a much different feeling for the politics at the top of the company than those at the client level.

Two weeks passed at my own rehab facility, and although my start date was only a week away, I'd heard nothing from the human resources department regarding pay, benefits, or anything at all. I became increasingly tense.

I convinced some of my friends at rehab to do some checking for me. Prudence made a call, and the regional marketing director's boss and the national marketing director called me shortly thereafter.

I was shocked to learn that he knew nothing about me. He seemed perplexed and refused to acknowledge I'd been hired. There was contempt in his voice when I said I'd be working in a new arm of the marketing department. He made it clear it was his marketing department, and there was no way he'd commit to me being hired in it. Huh? How could the regional marketing director have gone through all those meetings, given me that start date, and still not have mentioned me to the national marketing director? What was going on here?

He said he'd need to talk with the owner and also the regional marketing director to get up to speed on what had been discussed.

This was clearly going to set me back—two months back, to be exact.

In the meantime, I was going broke. I had a mortgage to pay, but no income other than what came from my settlement, much of which had already gone to my rehab facility. What was left was bleeding away while I waited.

Eventually he called me back, which was a relief. The owner had told him I did have a job, so we began talking about job duties. Sadly, the innovative media plans I'd suggested got mysteriously swept away. I'd be folded under the old marketing arm in such a way that there'd be no aggressive media push. He wondered what pay I expected to make. I asked for whatever was fair for a marketing position of this type, but he offered nothing, instructing me to make my salary demand. I did some research and decided on an entry-level marketing salary from which to prove myself. He felt it was too high. I asked him to counter. But an odd thing was happening. It seemed I had to reconvince him to hire me. I was getting fearful and told him my future there seemed in trouble. He assured that it wasn't and that this would all be resolved soon.

I soldiered on, but the two additional months stretched into three. All I wanted was to go to work and reach people like me who were in need of help. If my media plan had to wait, then so be it. I'd prove myself until then. I just wanted to do the work. In the meantime, I needed to make a living. The thought never occurred to me to look for another job, even as a backup. I'd been offered the job by the owner of the company, for goodness' sakes. Who was going to outrank him? Regardless, it felt cruel that they were stringing me along and not simply honoring the promise he'd made to me by getting me in there to work. I longed for the kindness I'd found out on Route 66 the previous year. This would have definitely never happened there; the people were so good-hearted. There was an old-time decency that prevented this sort of thing among people like that, but I was clearly a long way from that mentality now. I suddenly wished I could escape out there again.

But I needed work. There was no escaping that.

I called the national marketing director back at my own rehab and told him humbly that the length of time they were taking was becoming financially painful. After the June seminar I'd spoken at, I'd been hired by the owner in July, given a start date of September 1, and it was now late October. I still wasn't working and had no encouragement on the horizon. Three days later, he called to apologize.

He was saying he was sorry, but his tone didn't match the words. It was cold. Superior. Like a cat toying with a mouse. He was enjoying himself. He told me they'd finally resolved my position, pay, and benefits.

They'd decided to pass on hiring me.

I could almost see his satisfied grin on the other end of the phone.

I went in my room and fell on my bed, totally emotionally exhausted. I was most likely going to lose my house. What could I do? I decided to e-mail the owner and plead with him to rethink this decision.

His response? Indifference.

He never even returned my e-mail.

I was instantly transported back to that feeling of losing my job at the production company after the accident. My boss had decided I didn't have the skill set there, either. The big difference? Back then, he was right. That wasn't the case now.

Just as I'd been to the woman in the rehab supply room who'd spoken so differently after learning I'd been a patient there, I was "less" to them. All that was missing this time was the loud, slow talk. It was totally devastating, and I was completely flattened. I felt like a big loser. And again, for the first time in a long time, something else:

I felt brain-damaged.

But out of that experience came a startling discovery. I realized that although I was upset with the situation, I'd handled my emotions, sensitive emotions at that, with extreme control. The rages I'd experienced and expected while still going through my rehab were not happening. In that way, the whole experience might have been the most positive thing that could have happened to me.

I had just passed my final exam.

Twenty-Seven

~

"After the Storm"

IT WAS RIGHT AROUND THE TIME of my rehab's decision not to go forward that Kenny Langie, my old friend from Royal Family Kids' Camp, called. He'd wanted to check up on me.

I began to question whether God wasn't trying to guide me in which way to go. Maybe instead of reaching the end of the road with rehab, I'd been on the wrong street. I wondered: Was I supposed to be on a completely different road in life?

I called Kenny back. He thought I should be back in the field working with kids. I asked whether he really believed what he was saying about me. Basically, I really needed to hear it.

Kenny couldn't have been more supportive. He started praising my good heart and saying just how much difference he'd seen me make in the lives of the kids I'd worked with at camp the last few years. It so "happened" that his agency was hiring at that time, and his reputation was good enough that he "might" be able to get me in. He told me to send him my résumé, and that's just what I did. The very next day I got a call to interview. It was one of those "Can it be that simple?" moments. The answer was "yes."

Amazingly enough, I got that job working with kids on the same day of the interview. If they were abused kids, abandoned kids, neglected kids, foster kids, or kids at risk for involvement with the legal system ... I'd be their guy.

Was I sad not to be going over to the world of rehabilitation? Absolutely.

At the end of the day, though, the fact that I had all these great kids to work with each day sort of cushioned the blow. These kids regularly drank up the attention and compassion I had for them. The cool thing was that I got to work with teenagers too, so I could now expand my scope to kids a little older than those at Royal Family Kids' Camp.

It was also an exercise to see if I still had "the touch" in the psych field I'd had when I was a twenty-four-year-old wonder kid just snagging his master's degree. Ultimately, I also committed myself to not giving up on my goal of making an impact in the field of TBI, so I started coming up with an alternative plan going forward.

It might seem industrious for someone with my brain-rattled history, but I decided I'd work for one year with these kids, and if all went well, I'd make plans to go back and finish my doctorate.

That's right. The brain-damaged guy wanted to finish his doctorate.

What better way to inspire other victims than if one of their own showed the potential that still exists after injury by getting a PhD? In the meantime, after being out of the field for so long, I'd see to it that I recovered all those lost licensing hours and possibly, just maybe, I could take a shot at getting back to working with TBI patients as a doctor who knew their issues like no other. I'd be the guy they could talk to when they needed someone because I knew what it was like to not have support in recovery, and I knew the difference of having it later, as I'd had with Tammy at rehab. I knew that support and a listening ear were imperative. Kindness makes all the difference in the world to someone when you don't know where else to find it.

Actually, kindness makes all the difference in the world—period. It doesn't matter who you are or what you're dealing with. Kindness can change the world. I'd seen a lot of kindness and trust placed in me during my recovery, and now I'd be able to give it to others to see if it would make a difference in their lives as it had in mine.

A year later, right on the button, I began looking at the possibility of returning to graduate school. Things had worked out, and I was doing well with my clients, so, coming full-circle, I went right back to my old university—Alliant International University—and decided to proceed with my plan. Conveniently enough, Alliant now had a campus only an hour from my home in L.A. It made complete sense that through this whole crazy life journey from "therapist-to-be" to movie business hopeful and right back to doctoral work, I'd complete the circle by finishing the whole process at Alliant.

I didn't even apply anywhere else.

You may be surprised to hear that even though I'd had a great record, reputation, and grade point average when I attended previously, I still faced the same uphill battle of once again proving my "skill set" to the admission panel when I got to the interview stage of the process. They wanted to know, "Was grad school a good fit" for me now that I was brain-injured? Could I handle the work? On two separate occasions, I was told that the program was far more rigorous than it had been previously. They erroneously wondered whether I'd be able to handle all the class work and reading in my condition.

I told them after what I'd been through in rehab, I thought their program was going to be a piece of cake. I knew what it was when I'd been in it the first time, and even if it was more difficult, it'd be nothing compared to relearning to read at age thirty-three. I said I ultimately wanted to make a difference in the lives of TBI patients who were desperately in need of support and a listening ear. Moreover, with a PhD, I'd have the academic credibility to kick open doors in the field of brain injury that no one else had even approached. I couldn't wait to get started.

They turned me down flat.

Off the record, they told me a number of things, one of which was that I wasn't a "good fit" with my desire to work in the field of brain injury. I wondered what they had against it, but I didn't get the chance to ask. They also said that due to the "rigorous nature" of the program, I might not be good doctoral program material, considering that I'd had brain damage.

I'd been told point-blank by the program director that they'd once had a student who suffered a brain injury while attending their program, and his abilities afterward had never fully recovered. I said I believed that 100 percent, especially if he never got any rehab, but he probably could have gotten right back up to bat if he'd just gotten help. If he had, he'd have likely knocked it out of the park, and they'd have learned something about the potential for recovery from a brain injury. We just have to be given a chance.

One of my old professors was livid when he learned they'd turned me down. He told me that the Americans with Disabilities Act (ADA) protects TBI patients from being denied opportunities because of our conditions. Personally, I never labeled myself as disabled, and I still don't. If we're going to fail, though, this act gives us the opportunity to do it on our own rather than having someone deny us the opportunity before we even try. The university probably thought they were protecting me from crashing and burning, but truthfully, if I'm going to crash and burn, I'd rather be flying the plane myself than simply sitting there as a helpless passenger. Anyhow, my old professor was furious and stated that because of the ADA, they'd put themselves in a tenuous position. He reviewed my past history and wanted me to consider suing the school.

I never even had to consider it. Probably realizing the university's ADA violation, the program director decided to offer me the chance to come to the school anyway, to their esteemed main campus in San Diego, the same campus where I'd received my master's degree all those years ago. I told him I lived in L.A., and an impractical uprooting of my life or a 130-mile one-way drive to class wouldn't be convenient. That's why I'd applied to their Irvine campus.

Still, he said he'd love to have me in San Diego and didn't rule out that they might reverse their decision in Irvine if I wrote them a letter. You and I both know that I didn't really need to write that letter. Their knowledge of their error and ADA violation sealed that. So, without even writing the letter, I had my invitation back to school.

After thinking about it for a bit, I decided not to go. Here's why. Their rejection of me at Alliant had taken me back in time. At the time of my accident, all those years ago, with my master's degree and half of a completed doctorate under my belt, I'd had no clue about help for my recovery. Their teaching had been incomplete and was therefore useless to me at the time I needed it most. All these years later, they'd shown me again that many professionals in the psych field still have no clue about brain injury. Even professors. It was a wake-up call.

I was in a position where I'd moved forward and learned something that they still hadn't. Would I really have learned by studying under a group of people who had an obsolete understanding of TBI? No.

Do I still think there's a need for TBI patients to have therapists who truly understand their need for support and understanding? Of course! But you don't need a doctorate for that, just a license. Did I want to waste my time on a program stuck in past understandings or obsolete ways of thinking about brain injury? No way. Instead, I needed to rethink my future goals.

This is exactly why many TBI patients hide their conditions from the world. Victims know that mental deficiency isn't a selling point in getting ahead. Just because they're damaged doesn't mean they were born yesterday. They know from all the jokes and innuendos they've picked up on throughout their lives that mental impairment will get them judged, tossed away, and forgotten.

Instead of admitting there's a problem and getting help for it, they hide it to uselessly soldier on alone, waiting for a miracle recovery that will never come. Thus begins the inevitable cycle into the mental hell that in some cases is impossible to recover from.

Twenty-Eight

~

"Desert Angel"

OVER THE YEARS, I've driven Route 66 many times, always looking for the *Life* magazine spot, the place my dad and I had never found. Many years after Dad and I drove 66 together, I found myself in Seligman, Arizona, on the recommendation of John Harvey, a Route 66 friend of mine from Winslow, Arizona.

John shared with me that as a boy he'd ridden his bike up and down Route 66 through Arizona making grocery deliveries to families. Thinking he was probably the best resource I'd ever have to help me find the elusive Life magazine spot, I described to John what my dad and I had seen back in '85. I then saw something really cool. John closed his eyes and must have transported himself back in time fifty years along Route 66. He started describing the topography of the land in the photo. He remembered every curve in the road from his years on it, and when he opened his eyes, he thought he'd located that spot in Seligman, Arizona. He recommended that I stop into Angel Delgadillo's barbershop. He said Angel had lived on 66 his whole life, and he'd know where to find what I was looking for.

When I rolled into town, it was getting dark, and I'd nearly given up trying to find the spot in the road John had described. Something weird happened to me there, though, because in the early starts of the night, even though I couldn't see everything around me, I got to a spot in town next to a new post office that called out for me to stop. For some reason, something came over me that told me this was it. I'd reached the right spot in the road. It didn't look the same, especially in the encroaching darkness, but there was an energy in the air like the spirits of the natives telling me, "Yes, you can rest ... you've made it."

In the distance, but immediately in front of me, I saw something that looked, after all the years of searching, like I was right. Yes, there was the new post office, but just beyond that was a long rock wall. That wall, I was certain, had once stood in front of the West End Garage I remembered from the old photo. This had to be it, and if it wasn't it, I couldn't understand how such a match could exist and still not be the right place. How could I have missed all the correlations to the photo before? I looked at the contour of the road and the way it raised away from me into the distance. I could see burned-out old lights in an abandoned lot that undoubtedly illuminated several gas pumps in the distant past. The pumps were gone, but those lights, now unrecognizable to a casual passerby, were clearly the lights that had lit the gas station in the picture. They had to be.

The thing is, I had never conceived of heading east while looking for that *Life* magazine spot before, because classic 66 travel involved people heading west. I naturally guessed that the picture would accurately reflect that chapter in our country's history.

I went another mile down to Angel's barbershop to confirm it, and as I entered his shop, I saw a sight that nearly stopped me in my tracks.

It was a copy of the old photo from that *Life* magazine cover.

I hadn't seen it in years, and suddenly, there it was. That picture represented so much to me. Beyond my map appreciation of traveling our country as a kid, that picture had started my whole fascination with specifically exploring Route 66, and it had propelled me out on the road many times over the years in a quest to answer my dad's old question of what it looked like now. It had represented an escape to me, and it symbolized simpler times that were still full of promise in this country. I'd been searching for that promise in my own life since becoming disillusioned as a kid and witnessing all the chaos that had ensued since. I'd been searching for that promise since my accident had reinforced the chaos that had stripped my life as an adult.

Here I was, standing in front of the picture that I was sure had been taken just up the road, a road that had led to so much freedom and fun and friendship in my life in the years since.

I'd first seen this shot on that fateful trip with my dad in 1985 when it was revealed what had originally broken the peace in his family. Somehow for me, that picture had also come to represent the other side of a chasm created between him and my grandparents "somewhere on Route 66" all those years before. On one side was everything good, and on the other, everything that had been changed. Everything about my dad's life had changed on Route 66. And because it had, so, too, had mine, in a sense.

In a strange way, I owed my life to Route 66 because that trip had eventually been the catalyst that led my dad away from a life he wanted to escape before arriving in Flint and meeting my mom. His "escape" had given me the opportunity to grow up in what had once been the magnificence of the auto industry. Growing up in Flint had created in me a passion for America and for the plight of what had happened to our country and its citizens. Strangely, that picture had been taken in the very year my dad was born, and so it seemed linked with him. Suddenly, that picture seemed like it had something in common with the trains. It was another time machine capable of going back before things went ka-blooey in the Rice family. In that sense, it seemed possible of also being used to go back and make every-thing good again if a bridge could somehow be built to the other side.

As I stood there looking at the big framed photo, a train whistle blew in the distance. That seemed significant, and immediately off to my left, I saw a pleasant older man who looked to be somewhere in his sev-enties. He greeted me with a big, warm smile, and I asked him if the *Life* magazine shot had been taken in Seligman.

He explained it had been taken about a mile west down near the post office, in fact.

It was Angel Delgadillo I was talking to, and I hadn't even noticed that he'd been standing there with a younger woman behind the counter, his daughter Mirna. I introduced myself and they introduced themselves, and a stillness captured the moment that created a snapshot in my memory.

The train whistle tooted again, and it was almost as if Grandpa Goss was emphasizing the moment from Heaven for me. "Pay attention, Danny ... this is an important moment. You'll want to remember it."

I'd found the spot I'd been searching for so many years for and had just gotten confirmation from the man John Harvey had told me about, Angel Delgadillo. It seemed significant that my quest to answer my dad's old question about what that spot looked like would end up leading me straight to the very man in the town that I'd learned had eventually saved Route 66. It felt like a baton was being handed off toward something big-ger, only in a moment like that, you can't tell what it is ... you just hope you don't drop the baton.

I didn't want to lose whatever significance the moment was trying to communicate, so I talked with them both for quite a while. Without my asking, Mirna pointed out in the photo the rock wall I'd seen beside the road, and she shared how you could still see it if you were looking east.

Since I needed a haircut anyway, I asked if Angel would cut my shaggy head. He was only too kind to do it, and as he did, I told Angel some of the stories I'd heard about him.

I'd learned that when the government was preparing to bypass Route 66 with the interstate system, it was Angel who had the courage to stand up and protest. He told them what they were doing was wrong. By building a highway with no exits to any of the towns on old Route 66, he worried that they'd turn these towns into ghost towns and put hardwork-ing Americans out of work. These people, he reasoned, were the people who helped build this country by opening up the Southwest for easy explo-ration. In the process, Route 66 had become the backbone of the country. How could the government reward these good people for all their patrio-tism by mortally wounding them? How could they do this to such fantastically patriotic people?

I understood Angel completely. I'd watched the same thing happen to the good people of Flint, Michigan.

But the government didn't listen to Angel when he appealed to them, and the interstate opened as planned. For ten long years, he and the people of Seligman and all along Route 66 watched as the route started to die. They learned what it felt like to be forgotten. Angel watched as businesses closed and people he cared about had to move away. As I sat there in his barber chair, he told me how upset that had all made him. In that moment, I felt a kinship with Angel that I'd never expected. I'd lived the same life he had while I was growing up in Michigan, but several years removed. We had the same heart and the same passions. We believed in the same things. We cared about people, and we cared about America.

At the same time that Angel's plea for Route 66 and its people was being ignored by the powers that be in the name of "progress," a funny and unexpected thing began happening in the state capitals. The state tax revenues had started to die in conjunction with all those old towns, and suddenly, the very governments that had ignored the needs of Route 66 and continued to put all these people out of business realized they needed those same businesses they'd helped bankrupt to stay alive. What to do?

While Angel was steaming in Seligman, the state governments were panicking. They needed those tax dollars to keep running their states, but they had no idea how to resurrect a route they'd never known or appreciated in the first place. Angel had an answer for them. He'd form the "Historic Route 66 Association" and be the first president there in the little town of Seligman.

In 1987, Angel got the Arizona legislature to designate and preserve Route 66 in Arizona as a historic highway. From that point, other states along Route 66 followed his lead, and suddenly a movement had begun. Route 66 was resurrected and reborn, but make no mistake about it, it was Angel who saved it, and Angel who can be credited with "fathering" it back to health today.

Twenty-Nine

~

"Driving My Life Away"

Whedar A FRIEND OF MINE questioned why I was so fascinated with Route 66, we drove to Illinois so I could show him. He seemed to be enjoying himself, and for him, it was about discovering the road for the first time. For me, at least on this trip, I had a different mission in mind. After all these years of traveling it, I simply wanted to buy a T-shirt that said "Route 66" on it. Sounds simple, right?

It wasn't. Since I was raised in the Midwest, I'd been taught to buy American and support American workers. Therefore, I wasn't looking for just any T-shirt. I was looking for a T-shirt that was made in the USA. In 1985, when I'd first traveled the road with my dad, everything along the road was made in the USA. In 1992, it wasn't quite the case, and by the early 2000s, finding anything along the road that was American made was nearly impossible.

To search and not find a good American-made T-shirt on a road as American as Route 66 seemed ridiculous. So on the way back from Chicago, I searched the entire route, completely determined to find a quality shirt I could wear that would market my love for the Route, America, and what I believed this country once stood for.

Through Illinois there was nothing, and through Missouri there was nothing. Kansas you could forgive because it's only 13.2 miles of 66, but in Oklahoma, where you're really in the heartland, I was surprised not to find one. I was sure that in Texas, of all places, I'd be able to find one because what typifies the renegade, bucking bronco spirit of America better than Texas. Guess what? There was nothing.

By the time I got through New Mexico and Arizona, the writing was on the wall, but I was sure that at the end of Route 66, largely believed to be on the Santa Monica Pier in a spiritual, if not quite official, ending sense, I'd get the Route 66 shop there to sell me one. It's not what I wanted because, let's face it, I was now living in Los Angeles, and when you go on vacation, you don't want to buy a souvenir in your own town.

When I got to the pier, I was still empty-handed, but more than that I was mortified to find that after 2,448 miles and an amazing assortment of the best old-time diners, gift shops, museums, hotels, and Americans in our entire country, there was no Route 66 gift shop at its commonly accepted ending on the pier! How could that be?

I'd never noticed that, because in L.A., I wasn't trying to find or travel on Route 66 … I was trying to live my daily life. No, when I was on vacation or driving on Route 66, I was always heading out of L.A. toward the Mojave Desert and the Arizona border beyond it. I'd just never noticed that there was no shop on the Santa Monica Pier, let alone an American-made T-shirt for the road on the Santa Monica Pier. The fact that I couldn't find either felt like such a smack in the face to the Americans who'd kept the route alive for so many years since her decommissioning. How could this be?

I searched the shops that did exist with the thought that whether or not a shop was specifically a Route 66 shop, there might be a place that'd sell me an American-made Route 66 T-shirt. Guess what?

Nothing.

Instead, between a couple of shops, I found some bumper stickers and a Route 66 thimble. A Route 66 thimble?

It didn't make sense and it was disgusting to me. This road had always represented the best our country had to offer, and now it had been reduced to a thimble and a couple of stickers on a pier. The Santa Monica Pier was supposed to be the exclamation point on a 2,448-mile-long sentence, and all I was finding was a big fat raspberry.

How could it be possible that at the Santa Monica Pier, an iconic symbol of the past, present, and future greatness of the USA, there was no shopkeeper who understood the tremendous history of the "Mother Road" and the responsibility of holding up the torch of our country to the millions of tourists who visited from abroad each year?

Someone needed to open the granddaddy of all shops on the Santa Monica Pier to sell American-made T-shirts and to honor Route 66. I didn't mean me, of course, because I certainly couldn't afford it, but it seemed to be such a huge opportunity for the right company to capitalize on. It still is. The opportunity to promote and hold the torch for the USA. Who wouldn't want that? It was even more ironic that I was standing on the pier lamenting the loss of our country's knowledge of itself on a day that was a complete contradiction to what it stood for.

Almost unbelievably, it was the Fourth of July.

Thirty

~

"Born in the U.S.A."

BACK ON THE ROAD a year later, my Route 66 experiences took an irrevocable turn in August of 2005. That's because early in the morning on August 3, I was saddened to receive a call from my dad in Michigan telling me my Grandpa Rice had just passed away.

My grandpa had given me a lot in life, but more than anything, he'd always given me a quiet support to simply just be me. He believed in me, and I always felt it.

As I thought about our relationship, it was a bit funny that one of the things Grandpa and I started talking about a lot during my teenage years was marriage. Here was a man who had been married for sixty-one years and, beginning during my teenage years—when I had a girlfriend at the ripe old age of thirteen whom I was ga-ga about—he extolled the virtues of marrying the right woman and not being in a rush to get married. He stressed that this kind of partnership would be the most important one I'd ever form, and while the right one could be the best thing I might ever do for my life, the wrong one could absolutely destroy me. Annihilating myself was something that in my girl-crazy fever, he probably wanted to help me avoid.

I mention this because it wasn't long after he passed that I suddenly felt like I was getting help from up above in this department. In 2007, I met a woman like no other before her.

I was at a going-away party for a friend of mine in Santa Monica when I spotted this attractive blonde woman, literally, from across a crowded room. A friend asked me what I was looking at, and I pointed her out.

"I'm your wing-man and I'm going in," he said, and he made a beeline for her table. Ten minutes later, I was talking with one of the most gentle, sweet-spirited, kind women I'd ever spoken to. Jessica had a faith in God, and she was from Michigan like me but lived in Los Angeles. She'd worked in the movie business for a bit, but like me, she'd also left it behind. We'd gone to the same university in Michigan and we'd moved to California at the same age. The similarities only began there. I told her I felt like I was talking to the female version of myself, and somehow I worked out a planned abandonment from my buddy so I could try to manage a ride home from Jessica.

When she dropped me off that night, I didn't waste time. I took her out to dinner the next night. Soon after that, I had her out on Route 66 for her first time, and you knew it was serious if I was doing that.

A year after we began dating, in early 2008, I told her of a plan I had for an old railroad hotel in Seligman, Arizona, called the Havasu. I wanted to restore it, run it, and dedicate a room to honor Angel Delgadillo right there in his hometown. I also wanted to check out Jessica's interest in this plan because losing a woman who was so precious wasn't something I was willing to do, and committing to this plan would obviously involve relocation from California.

To my great pleasure, the idea of watching the sun go down each night from the veranda of our restored hotel beside Route 66 and the railroad was one she could get behind. The irony that I might end up in the same town where the *Life* magazine cover shot was taken seemed like no cosmic accident. I felt bound to Route 66 somehow, and it felt like a natural thing that our paths were converging there.

That's why I was surprised a few months later when we returned to look at the hotel. After so many years in Seligman, the Havasu had been completely leveled—there was not even a clue that it once stood there.

I joked to Jessica that it was clear God didn't want me in Seligman. He'd been pretty quick about demolishing the Havasu after I started showing such serious interest in leaving California and moving there. For so many years of it standing so stoically, and literally two months after she and I had the conversation about buying it, the Havasu was gone.

It was strange, and yet, something had me questioning whether I'd failed. Maybe if I'd moved my life's journey closer to Route 66 when I was younger, I could have avoided a brain injury, and the Havasu could have been saved after all. Nevertheless, it was gone.

A couple hours later, Jessica and I were just outside of Flagstaff. I was in exactly the westernmost spot I'd been in with my dad back in 1985 during my first Route 66 trip when my cell phone rang.

It was Dad. This time he told me that Grandma Rice was having some health difficulties. In fact, she'd fallen and broken her hip and had required extensive surgery to try to put it back together. It was an extremely bad break, and despite the surgery, things didn't look good.

Just two and a half weeks later, and only two and a half years since losing Grandpa Rice, she followed him into Heaven. It was a little unbelievable, considering that just a year earlier, she'd been driving me around town in her sporty, new fire-engine red Chevy Impala. Barely a year later, she was gone.

Their successive losses in such a short time affected me pretty deeply. These two had always been the celebrity couple that wowed me with their experiences in the big city of Chicago. They'd given me stability in a time I desperately needed it. They also showed me that it was possible to live out of state from your family and still maintain a loving relationship with them. I'd certainly come to perpetuate their example in living that out. More than that, they'd reinforced the feeling that I could do anything, the same feeling I'd had when racing the trains with my dad and mom all those years before. They'd affected my life as much as anyone.

I was sad that somehow we'd never gotten to the point where an apology had been made between them and their sons for that Route 66 surprise move back in the 1960s, but in the forty-some years since it had happened, I guess it didn't matter so much to any of them anymore. Dad had told me he didn't lament the life he'd lived, and Uncle Larry had no complaints from raising a beautiful family of three fun girls with my Aunt Linda.

Still, I wished for at least some admission to their sons that they'd made a mistake back then, just to clear away that sad bit of history for good and any miniscule regrets that may have lingered between them. To me, that whole episode and the indifferent pain it had caused was simply so unnecessary. All four of them were amazing people, and an apology would have gone a long way, in my opinion. But they'd already made such a great recovery. Perhaps it was a moot point.

It wasn't long after that I was informed by my Uncle Larry that my grandparents had set a small amount of money aside for each of the grand-children, and I'd be receiving mine soon. All us grandkids were encouraged to invest it, and the thought was that it could possibly grow into something much more. My grandpa, who loved investments and the financial world, would have loved that.

I had a slight problem with this, though. This money represented what was left of my grandparents. Simply putting it in some anonymous stock that could go belly up at any time wasn't that appealing to me. It was a small enough amount that it wasn't going to buy much, and if it was go-ing to represent the last gift they ever gave me, I wanted to make it count. Having an anonymous stock go bust one day wasn't what I wanted to have happen if it was going to be my last tie to them because in that way, my time with them would have truly been over.

I wanted to figure out some investment that would be a testament to the lives they'd lived. I wanted it to be something that could grow and extend the goodness of their lives beyond their years—something that truly represented them. I'd be extremely limited in what I could do, and it would clearly have to be something on a smaller scale. What could I do, what could I do?

My wheels were spinning. While he was in Chicago, my grandpa had worked for the Department of Labor in the Wage Hour Division. What this meant was that he'd always fought for the little guy. Grandpa Rice made sure that the rank-and-file, blue-collar guy on the line was getting paid and treated well by his employer, so it wasn't the employer my grandpa represented. No, my grandpa was advocating for the working man against bosses who weren't always so fair.

I tried to think if there was anything I could do that might honor the working man he'd fought so long and hard for. I'd need to think about it.

Because he was working in the '60s, '70s, and '80s, my grandpa had been plenty busy during the demise of the manufacturing era I'd grown so disturbed by. Was there anything going on during that time that might also represent him?

My wheels kept turning. Sure there was. Route 66. My grandpa had lived in Chicago. Right there at the start of it. I lived in L.A. at the end of it now, but I'd gotten my start on Route 66 with him there in Chicago. The road linked both our histories. In between it, "somewhere on Route 66," my *whole family*'s course had been radically changed. There had to be something I could do on Route 66 that would link all our history and do something positive for my grandparents' legacy and the road at the same time. Where was there a need that could use a little of Grandpa Rice's investment and also do good for the people on Route 66?

That's when it struck me. I lived in L.A., and at the end of the road, in all of its history, *there had never been a Route 66 shop on the Santa Monica Pier!*

I already knew the shop's main product. Route 66 and this country needed a high-quality *American-made T-shirt!* One that promoted Route 66 and America from the Santa Monica Pier. It made total sense!

It would put American workers back to work, help Route 66, improve the economy of our country, and be a tip of the hat to my grandpa's defense of the little guy all at the same time.

Then something *really* started tingling in my head. Here was my dad, who had been completely wounded and rerouted on Route 66, and for what purpose?

Twenty-five years earlier, he'd passed on that story to me, and if you don't believe in coincidence, then that revelation had to have been for a grander purpose. It meant I'd seen that *Life* magazine photo *for a reason* all those years before. I could use that photo like a "time machine" to link me back to any mistakes my grandparents might have made, and I could finally make them right.

I'd been perfectly placed by God to make any of the hardship my dad had gone through count for something. I realized that I was probably the only one on the planet who could have been born to do that in this way. What a gift from God!

If my dad realized the implications that what he went through back then, all those decades before, was going to finally lead to something that would put Americans back to work, support the American economy, and champion its history from a forum as grand as the Santa Monica Pier, he'd most likely flip. He was always the guy who'd take it on the chin for you. To know that he'd gone through the sometimes less than stellar upbringing he experienced in the '50s and '60s so that his *unborn son* could later do something to help Route 66 *and* the USA would most likely do more than just make that early '60s trip right for him. It would justify his whole life with my grandparents, and because of their seed money to start my company, they'd be indirectly responsible for making it all happen. They'd be responsible for healing the situation with Dad. Even after their passing, this company would still be a family operation that took all of us in our victories and our defeats together to make happen. I loved that.

I INCORPORATED MY T-SHIRT COMPANY "66-to-Cali, Inc." in the summer of 2008. Soon after, with Jessica at my side, I went about the big job of finding the right manufacturing partner for the good-quality American-made Route 66 shirts that we were going to found our company on.

In the fall of '08, I found my friend John. He was making shirts in downtown L.A. and employed about seventy-five American workers at his small factory. All I needed was the additional capital necessary to make my first run of shirts with him. Thanks to Grandpa Rice, I had it.

We spared no expense and used the finest-quality cottons we could, straight from Georgia, so Americans there could benefit too. After all, I figured if we're going to make a T-shirt in the USA, we wanted the American one to be the best one, and we wanted customers to feel the difference in our quality.

By March of 2009, we'd completed our first run of "Historic Route 66" T-shirts. There were a thousand of them to start, just enough to test the market.

With no appointments and a truck stuffed with new T-shirts, but no Santa Monica store yet to sell them from, Jessica and I set off toward Chicago. I'd focused on fifteen landmark locations on Route 66 that we'd need to market to, all of which were of the caliber to handle the high-quality T-shirts we'd made and would definitely cater to a crowd that appreciated "Made-in-the-USA" products.

When we reached Chicago, the city where it all began, I gazed up at the John Hancock Building. It had represented so much strength to me throughout my life and so much stability with my grandparents that even being near it again was magical. It had been my "home away from home," and it felt good to be "home" again. We spent a few days drinking up the ambience of the city and meeting with people about our shirts.

Several times a day, I walked past my grandpa's old workplace and gazed up at where his office had been. For a moment, I could feel him there with me, encouraging me, proud of me. I felt the presence of Grandma Rice walking with me along the streets she'd toured me around so many times before. There was the legendary Berghoff Restaurant and Miller's Irish Pub. The Palmer House Hotel. I felt one with it all and, like that first time racing the train with Dad and Mom as a child, like I could do anything. Before we left, I had "66-to-Cali" T-shirts right there on the very corner of Michigan

Avenue and Adams ... the very beginning of westbound Route 66 in Chicago and a few steps from my grandpa's old building. It felt completely right.

By the time we got back to L.A., a wild thing had happened. Of the fifteen Route 66 landmarks we'd targeted across the country to sell our shirts from, not one of them turned us down. They all simply stated they hadn't been able to get American-made products anymore. They were so happy we'd found them! Somehow, unbelievably, between March 29, 2009, and April 7, 2009, I went from working in social services to owning an already successful and burgeoning Route 66 T-shirt company!

I'd like to say that it was all because of the hard work Jessica and I put in, but the truth is, we didn't feel like we were alone on the trip. To the contrary, we both believed God was with us because along the way, we "just happened" to bump into the director of the Route 66 Alliance, Jim Conkle, who incidentally lives two thousand miles away but "just happened" to be at the same Ariston Café in Litchfield, Illinois, where we "just happened" to be eating our dinner. That's just too much coincidence for a guy like me who doesn't believe in it.

The owner, Nick Adam, whom I'd met on a trip there once with my dad, offered to introduce me to Jim. You know the rest. Jim loved our shirts, and he was so completely generous and supportive of what we were trying to do. He offered whatever help he could give us, and after thanking him, we kept on our way with his number in our hands. We'd just gotten the blessing of the Route 66 Alliance's director.

It was like that the whole way. We'd walk into a place, and the owner or buyer for that particular outlet would be the first person we'd talk to. There were no coincidences here. It was the first time in my life that I could say I was exactly where God wanted me at exactly the right time. By the time we got back to L.A., our little Route 66 business was booming—thanks to God.

We just had one other problem. We needed a place to operate from in L.A.

I knew the need for a shop on the Santa Monica Pier because there'd never been one for me or any of the millions of others who had ended their Route 66 journeys there over the years.

We'd applied to the City of Santa Monica right before we left on our trip across America, and we'd been waiting patiently for a few months for an answer to our business proposal. By Memorial Day weekend, we got one.

To my utter surprise, we'd been turned down!

It didn't make sense at all, and while I was disappointed, I wasn't devastated because it oddly didn't feel like the end. Nothing about that decision against us made any sense with every door we felt God had already opened for us. It was no mistake that everywhere we went along the road, the owners or buyers for the places we went to just happened to always be the first people we'd meet inside the door. I'd said to Jessica that if I'd never had faith before, there was no way I couldn't have had it after that trip. It seemed God had gone before us and set up all the meetings, and we'd simply come in and close the deals He'd arranged. If He was that involved with us on our cross-country trip, then I knew there was a mistake made with turning down our pier store, but what could I do? Something was off, but it was way bigger than me, and I believed the only one big enough to change it was somebody up above.

I discussed it with Jessica, and we came to the agreement that God wasn't a God of chaos, and the last few months had been quite chaotic. It was possible He was simply giving us a break to get things in order. We'd get our wholesale business on the route more established, work on developing our website, and in six months, we'd apply for a vendor cart again. With that settled, Jessica and I were content.

Three weeks after getting the rejection, my phone rang. It was "Donna Rickman with the City of Santa Monica." She asked if I was still interested in putting "66-to-Cali" on the pier. I told her I was, and she told me I was being offered the vendor space I'd originally applied for.

Suddenly, "66-to-Cali" was the first shop in nearly eighty-three years to ever operate an exclusive Route 66 shop at the end of America's Main Street on the Santa Monica Pier. We would now be the only company in the world with our Route 66 T-shirts at the beginning, the middle, and the end of Route 66.

I then went about designing a proper "End of the Road" T-shirt for all those annual travelers who begin on Route 66 in Chicago and who journey the full 2,448 miles before ending on the pier in Santa Monica. Certainly, now that there'd be an "end of the road" store, there needed to be an "end of the road" shirt. Only what would it look like?

I was bolted awake one night from a sound sleep with my company slogan on the pier. "End of the Road, Beginning of the Dream." It felt too divine to have come from my brain because it so perfectly summed up what the pier had symbolized for so many over the years.

I put that slogan on the back of the shirt with a beautiful illustration of the pier above it. On the front of the shirt, I was hoping for some sort of old classic signage I could include that would have not only Route 66 history but also something specific to the end of Route 66.

Because all the signage disappeared in Santa Monica when Route 66 was decommissioned, Jessica and I began searching through a bunch of old Route 66 photos. We were just beginning to give up when we came across one we'd never seen before. It was a simple sign and it was unique. It said three things: "Santa Monica. 66. End of the Trail." It was perfect.

I immediately called my new patent attorney and checked to see if anyone owned the image. Before our call was over, he'd filed the paperwork, and someone did. Me.

There was no way I could take the chance of not buying the rights to the sign's image and then have someone come along later and buy them from under me just to charge me to sell my shirts. The shirt wouldn't even have been possible to sell if I hadn't found the sign in the first place. With the rights to the image secured, I could proceed with creating my "End of the Trail" shirt with the "End of the Road, Beginning of the Dream" message on the back.

From the day we opened on July 30, we started selling so many of those shirts you'd have thought they were campfires at the North Pole. We were asked by the executive director of the pier at the time, Ben Franz-Knight, about the story of the sign on the shirt, and I told him the history I'd learned since first discovering it. The "End of the Trail" sign had originally been a prop movie sign, but it evolved into becoming the impetus for why Route 66 had been extended all the way to Santa Monica in the first place. It seems we'd been responsible for bringing it back ... if only on a T-shirt from our tiny beach shack on the pier.

But the story doesn't end there. After learning the sign's history and seeing how many "End of the Trail" shirts we were selling, Ben offered me the opportunity to put that old lost sign back up. Since I owned the sign's image, and he represented the city who owned the pier, it seemed we could do business. I had the sign reconstructed soon after, and exactly seven years and two days to the day after my car accident, on November 11, 2009, I got to resurrect that old "End of the Trail" sign on the Santa Monica Pier. Route 66 was back in a big way, and it seems ... so was I.

The sign went up that day in front of a horde of cameras, newspaper photographers, and radio announcers reaching sixty million people around the world. As I stood there marveling at it all, I couldn't help but realize that the "End of the Trail" meant something completely different to me than it had after my accident.

I thought my life was over back in 2002. It was anything but that now. Seven years later, every road that God had ever put me on, before or after my accident, finally converged at the Santa Monica Pier. It had begun in Chicago with my grandpa. It had continued with my dad during that first trip on Route 66 together in 1985. In 1992, God took me a little further down my life's journey when I traveled to California on it for grad school. Following my recovery in 2004, the Route 66 community embraced me again and allowed me the freedom to celebrate the life I'd just reclaimed. And finally, from that trip was born a dream to keep my grandpa and our family's legacy alive on Route 66.

On June 19, just ten and a half months after we'd opened, our little company "66-to-Cali" was given the Will Rogers "New Business of the Year" award for 2010 on Route 66, an honor that I still can't quite find words for. As a brain-injured guy who had been passed over and rejected more times than he could count for being damaged, the phenomenal suc-

cess of our first year was a little surreal. Unbelievable, even. Our little store and the work I'd done had marketed Route 66 to literally millions of people in a very short time. Not bad for a guy with no "skill set," eh?

A year to the day after Jessica and I took that original trip to get our T-shirts sold all along Route 66, we took another trip on it to touch base with all our friends along the way. In the year since we'd made that first trip together across the country as a couple, the series of events she and I'd experienced had turned out to be more amazing than either of us could have ever imagined. As a bonus to me, Jessica had turned out to be not just a great girlfriend but also such a great partner in the T-shirt business and everything I was trying to do for Route 66. Not only was she kindhearted and sweet, she'd shown herself to have a faith that was as important to her in her life as my faith is in mine.

Maybe not coincidentally, one of the fun roadside attractions on Route 66 in Texas is the "Largest Cross in the Western Hemisphere," so we stopped to visit it. Very near the midpoint of the entire road, this place captures everything I've ever thought was right about America. There's the rolling countryside, the small American town nearby, the big rigs carrying their loads on the interstate all within sight of the Cross, and good old Route 66 beside it, reminding us of a kinder, gentler time in our nation's history. And then, of course, at the center of all this quiet beauty is the Cross and the reminder of a God who is bigger than we are and always hoping to be at the center of our lives.

I asked Jessica to marry me that day in the quiet of Groom, Texas. With no one around but the two of us and the masterfully painted setting sun, the scene felt undoubtedly arranged by the God, whose Cross had been standing there behind us and yet had guided us through our whole relationship. She said yes, and just a few months later, we married in a small church ceremony with our families and a few close friends around.

On that day, it was clear. I'd gotten my life back. In blinding fashion.

~

The End.

For good quality American-made t-shirts go to www.66toCali.com.

LaVergne, TN USA
20 December 2010
209457LV00002BA/7/P